How The Hell Did You Do That?!

How The Hell Did You Do That?!

They forget, adversity births legends

By Octavia Yearwood

Octavia Yearwood
P.O. Box 370372
Miami, FL 33137
www.OctaviaYearwood.com

First printing, 2017
The New O Publishing
Book Layout by www.writingnights.org

ISBN 978-0-9989333-0-6

Ordering Information:

Quantity sales. Special discounts are available on quantity purchases by corporations, associations, and others. For details, contact the publisher at the address above.

Printed in the United States of America

"THE STONE THAT THE BUILDER REFUSE, WILL ALWAYS BE THE HEAD CORNERSTONE." – BOB MARLEY

This book is a manifestation of the guiding spirits. I am half author and whole messenger. Writing this was made possible by universal love.

THANK YOU-

Big love to the donors whose support allowed me to bring this physical book to your hands:

Harrison Cole & family, Que Harrison, Priscilla Alvarez, A C, Lynda Denver Bonaminio, Family Benmeleh, Tara Strickstein, and 44 others. THANK YOU!

Thanks to Lakiesha Foreman, the creator, and my grand-mother Amy Yearwood for inspiring me and supporting me through this process; this book would not have been without both of you.

Thanks to my sister, my nephews Arthur and Antaeus, and my nieces, Amy and Athena: your unconditional love has been the fuel I needed! I want the best out of this world for you! Auntie loves you endlessly.

Thanks to all of my friends who inspire change and make it happen; watching you all has been inspiring. Thanks to Nathan Blake, Yasmine Satici, Johnny J Hines III, Martine Harris, Miranda Canty, Laura Gandolfo & Family, and Nicole Russell for all your care and love, and for putting a roof over my head when I had none and for not expecting anything in return. I am forever grateful and I hope putting that in print proves that!

Thanks to the Nichols Family, Auntie Allison, and countless other people that believed in my potential far before I knew I had any.

Thanks to RichandLEX.com for believing in me, my vision and my quest to save the world, and for making so much happen for "The New O".

Thanks to my unofficial mentor, Tracey Robertson Carter, for pushing me hard and supporting me harder.

Thanks to every stranger that has smiled or made a nice gesture- because of you, humanity is better off.

Thanks to whoever is reading this book; you are supporting in saving the life of a foster child or any other child that needs it, and you are choosing to better your own.

<3 You are composed of the sum of things,

most of which are not filled with glitz, glam or supported wings.

While bound, you are free to go,

In a cage with open doors but nowhere to flow.

Corners bring you comfort like open arms,

Darkness brings opportunity in the inevitable light...

So Remember,

It's Gon Be Alright <3

~~TABLE OF CONTENTS~~

~~INTRODUCTION~~

Always pulling your insides out and tossing them onto the floor. Walking around like Frankenstein, you've reassembled yourself so many times.

Always going straight through because the other routes take longer. Always wondering if there's real worth in something so painful. Waiting for the new superpower to kick in at any moment, while continuing to grow a new understanding for avoidance everyday. The many selves kick it when they need to, pulling your soul to the finish line that also happens to be the start, again.

THIS is what you call, a win.

You're right, shit is hard. NO, it won't get easier. Yes, you will get stronger. You weren't born into comfort; you were created by many and probably cared for by less. Begin to tell yourself that this is okay because if you are reading this, you are on the right path. My inspiration to write this book was YOU. This book was made possible by the many who inspired me. The quotes you will see in this book are by real-ass people who, like you, have been through some real-ass shit.

Introduction

guide *(noun)*

    1. A person who advises or shows the way to others.

    2. A thing that helps someone to form an opinion to make a decision or calculation.

Constantly being disregarded, extremely mistreated, and feeling thrown away is something that could ruin you and cause you to ruin others for the rest of your life – only if you don't work through it. Adults seem to be in a whole other book when you're a young person. We assume they were never our age and never experienced anything remotely similar to what we're experiencing.

How could they be able to treat you the way they do if they had? Why don't they listen? Why don't they understand? They are only doing what they can do. Hopefully, what you will take away from reading this book is not only how to free yourself, to be better, and realize that you can have better, but also gain an understanding about all those who have wronged and abandoned you. Ideally, you will realize how much power you really have and how much power you unknowingly give away.

As a young person, you are the most amazing prize this world has. You make every adult important. Without you, they would have no reason to be here. You are the inspiration and cause for success. You Are Everything. Being an adult is actually an alter ego.

Is he Superman or Clark Kent? If you say he's both, you would be right, but if he never tapped into and accepted his "Super Self," who would save the world? Not Clark Kent! Clark Kent is the true alter-ego adult. He is nervous, awkward, and timid. He hides no one sees him. He yearns for things only because he convinces himself he could never have them. No one respects him. He doesn't even have perfect vision! He wears glasses! But as soon as he sheds all those lies, changes his clothes and steps into his greatness, magic happens. Not only does he save lives and bring safety and comfort to others, but he finds love! How rewarding life is when you are your true self. Imagine how far you can get and how much of an impact you can have when you never forget that you were born to be super. See, Superman may have also been Clark Kent, but he never forgot that there was also a Superman in him.

It's possible to grow up but not become an adult if this alter ego makes you forget who you really are and what you were meant to achieve here. It's a product of all the bad shit you experienced. It's who you create to protect you from being hurt again, being poor again, or being used again. The adult alter ego has pop-up blockers that keep you in a space of fear. Your Super Self doesn't live in that space.

It's likely that the last time you were your Super Self was when you were really young, somewhere between one to six years old. Then, slowly but surely, adult alter egos around you started to chip away at you, molding you into something else. With time, you started chipping away at yourself. You created these defenses and began using them on everyone except the alter egos that created you. You might find yourself getting in fights, stealing, lying, or cursing people out at the drop of a dime. You might even beat your significant other, and you might have even taken a life. Shit happens. The past is the past and you are only meant to pay for your mistakes once. The time to stop the patterns of pain is now. Every hurtful thing you do is a result of your past experiences, so let's make some new ones.

Introduction

I've spent a lot of time wondering why the hell I'm here, and why I had to hurt so much. Nearly every time I took the "high road," gave someone the "benefit of the doubt," or tried to "be nice," I was left feeling like I should've scrapped it and done them dirty. Maybe if I had responded truthfully, I would have felt better, but I'll never know. The one thing I do know for sure is that having control in these moments made me stronger in the next. I also believe that if I had responded truthfully in those moments where I chose to hide behind being nice, I wouldn't have met the many people on this earth who were sent to help and guide me.

I didn't just wake up in those situations, however. My mother was a crack head that left my sister and me in a crack house. Our grandmother, who shared these stories like family heirlooms, told us that when she found us at the crack house, we were dancing on a table in diapers. Consequently, I was a foster child who was never adopted and traveled from foster home to foster home with all my belongings in black garbage bags. My first foster home experience included me being forced to eat out of a dog's bowl. I was maybe 5 or 6 at the time, but old enough to vividly remember what had happened to me.

I'm currently on a flight from Boston back to New York, after receiving the 2016 American Express Emerging Leader Award from Americans For The Arts, a leading non-profit arts organization. I'm also writing my first book. If you decide that you are going to be and remain super, YOU WILL. Your eyes following my words on these pages is a confirmation of that. Surviving what I've been through means that I'm able to share my tragedies as well as my triumphs with you.

heir • loom *(noun)*
  A valuable object that is owned by a family for many years and passed from one generation to another.

Reading about my journey is completely useless unless it encourages you to examine your own. In order to do that, each chapter includes a workbook-type space for you. You can hide and lie to the world but you can't hide and lie to yourself. Sometimes in our effort to fool others we also fail to keep it real with ourselves. "Truth Through The Pen" is where you begin to identify your truth, get them out of your head, and see them out loud. Hopefully, you will discover that a lot of situations are less about the person or situation and more about your own perspective.

"YOU CANNOT BEHAVE APPROPRIATELY UNLESS YOU PERCEIVE CORRECTLY."- A COURSE IN MIRACLES

per • spec • tive: *(noun)*
  A particular attitude toward or way of regarding something; point of view.

I hope sharing my truths and stories will inspire and help you to realize your greatness.

I'm going to leave you with a mantra that I want you to revisit in those many moments of pain, aggravation, strife, anger and all other hopeless feelings.

man • tra *(noun)*
  A word or statement used and or repeated to bring you to a place of peace or harmony.

Introduction

"Imma Win Out This Bih!"

Imma win, Imma win, Imma win.

Every loss is a win,

Every win is a step towards another win.

Imma breathe right now (take a deep breath),

Because breath is life and if I'm livin' I'm winnin'.

All the challenges and blocks matter because you don't win without a challenge,

I accept that challenge.

In acceptance I win!

Adversity Births Legends.

Adversity Birthed Me,

Imma Win Out This Bih!

how THE hell did YOU do THAT?!

Use this to support yourself and the people around you. If you win they win, and if they win then you win.

Each day I work to provide the people around me with everything I once lacked. I give them beautiful words. I give them affection. I give them inspiration because I become the hope. I give everything I wish I once had. Everyday I am surprised by how much I get back from giving. Love was all I wanted growing up, love is all I focus on giving now, and love has proven to be all we really need.

ad • ver • si • ty *(noun)*

1. A state or instance of serious or continued difficulty or misfortune.

2. Unfavorable fortune or fate; a condition marked by misfortune, calamity, or distress.

I Love You, Yo! Read On.

Introduction

~~Presta Atención~~

"YOU CAN'T SELL DREAMS TO SOMEONE WHO HAS WALKED THROUGH NIGHTMARES..." - INSTAGRAM MEME

Life is a game. People always say it, and it's usually said in a way that makes you feel like you either need to manipulate it or not take it seriously. If you think about it, that doesn't explain a game at all. From Assassin's Creed to UNO, when you play, you're trying to win. It's conscious, it's strategic, it's serious sometimes, and it's fun sometimes. Most often, regardless of if you win or lose, you want to play again. Now that's more like life!

Like in a game, every time you feel good is because you've "won" or beat a level. However, the next level is likely to be harder and the chance of losing always increases. Just by simply trying again. This realization is the root of fear for most of us and ends up being the reason they never move into their Super Selves.

"OK, AND?"

Well, why did that happen? You have to ask yourself these questions. I'll give you a hint: it's NOT the game's fault. It's not the experience's fault either. Actually, I'm going to ask that you slowly begin to retire the word "fault" from your vocabulary. Don't give it to yourself or to anyone else. "Fault" is a black hole married to guilt and it will keep you DOWN. Once you give it or take it you slowly lose your ability to move on from the situation. Instead, you'll continue beating yourself up. "Fault" can easily turn into a reason why you believe you're not great. "Fault" drowns your ability to create, and yet your ability to create is all you have.

In intense moments, we are usually taught just how powerful words are by when and how we use them.

When I was younger, if I replied "what" to my parents (which I didn't because it was ingrained in me that it was very disrespectful), they would have automatically puffed out their chest and wondered if I had momentarily lost my mind. What is so wrong with "what"!? Why weren't my own feelings in that moment important? Maybe I was frustrated with school, work, or friend drama and you caught me at a bad moment. It didn't matter; "what" was a trigger that I wasn't allowed to pull. I too adopted that rule and saw a "what" response as disrespectful; until I didn't.

trig • ger *(noun)*
   1. To cause someone to have a particular feeling or memory.

Amongst a slew of other things like someone not returning a text or a friend jokingly calling me a bitch or goofy, I began to wonder why so many things would instantly set me off. Whether or not it was valid, I was still a slave to a list so many things that didn't actually cause me physical harm or threaten my life. I simply started thinking they weren't okay, and like magic they weren't. My head was on a swivel. Because of that,

how THE hell did YOU do THAT?!

I would engage in confrontation after confrontation...until I didn't.

Thoughts, though fleeting, can be one of the most powerful tools you have. Your thoughts create. They travel from the limitless space in your mind and go into the world. They play tag with people in your life; some you have yet to meet. Your thoughts are why you spill that juice you filled to the brim or not. Your thoughts are why that person you were just thinking about shot you a text or called you. Yes, it's when you think you're the best spades partner and mentally take the credit when your team wins.

Your thoughts are how you create the world around you. Everything in your life is meant to be there because it is serving you in some way. It's either helping to shape your thoughts or it's the result of your thoughts. These are the keys! You have to be fully aware of what is shaping your thoughts and what you are shaping with your thoughts.

a • ware *(adjective)*

1. Knowing that something (such as a situation, condition, or problem) exists.

2. Feeling, experiencing, or noticing something (such as a sound, sensation, or emotion).

3. Knowing and understanding a lot about what is happening in the world or around you.

Experiences shape your thoughts like a planted seed. It can be planted by anyone, and they don't even have to be significant to you. If a tourist steps on your foot and doesn't apologize, you may start thinking "all tourists are rude." Experiences are so lasting because all your senses are involved. Sights, smells, and sounds trigger emotions that are attached to your physical body. Your heartbeat rises, your stomach drops, you hold your breath—

Whatever it might be, it is very much real and active. You feel it. Learning to be aware of these chemical reactions in my body has been a major key to me becoming a better person and shaping the world around me.

See, when seeds are planted, our natural instinct is to feed it and let it grow. This is why seeds rooted in trauma, pain, aggression and other hindering energies draw in more experiences that are traumatic, painful and aggressive. Just like insects to plants, we are no different. Then things that were meant be a one time experience become our everyday experiences; from a lesson to a profession. We don't realize it until we do. Then we can start using our thoughts to shape the world around us, choosing and creating each moment the way we want them to be.

The first step, I've found, is to start digging up all the rooted seeds that no longer serve you. I started off small when I began exercising my right to choose, finding myself more and more empowered by choice. I said to myself "Okay, I'm not going to get angry anymore if my friend jokingly calls me a bitch." Then I told myself "Okay, I'm not going to feel hurt when my foster parents introduce me as their 'foster daughter.'" I just kept going, slowly breaking these rules I set that did nothing but hurt me and make my life more complicated. I gradually learned it wasn't the people that were hurting me, it was my thoughts about what they were saying that hurt me. I had to take responsibility for my actions, and more importantly, to take control of my experiences starting with my thoughts. The truth is that you can only win in life when you've won over your thoughts.

My Life

Around the ages of 5,6, or 7, [I really think the trauma of it is the reason why I can't pinpoint the age] I was mistakenly dropped into hot water and suffered 2nd degree burns all over my body. My sister and I were taken out of our grandmother's house and put into a foster home for the first time. My new foster mom made me eat out of a dog bowl, didn't allow me at the dinner table, and made me sleep on the floor. I remember at night sometimes my sister would try to get me to sneak into her bed with her. She felt bad that she was allowed to do things I wasn't, so she often invited me to join her, but I refused because I didn't want her to get into trouble.

When my sister told my grandmother, she petitioned to get us back and won. We weren't there for long, but for many years after that I couldn't even hear that woman's name. The story of what happened to us was on repeat in the coming years, but in four or five year's time I would be back in foster care... This time, it was by choice. I decided I didn't want to live with my grandmother anymore. I wanted a mother and a father. I was done with wearing thrift store clothes. In the end, I got what I wanted, along with a lot of what I didn't... I was only 11 years old but at least it was my choice.

<3 <3 <3

Presta Atención

Looking back, I see that choosing to go back into a foster home at 11 years old ended up becoming the catalyst for where I am now. I made a choice, and even though I had no plan, I had a vision. Unlike the first time, I knew my rights. I knew what they couldn't do and I knew I would make noise and make myself heard if they tried to wrong me. In retrospect, I realize if the first foster home didn't happen, I wouldn't have been prepared for the second time or for now. The shift in thought made all the difference; I didn't allow the first time to define my life. I used what I learned from it and placed myself in a situation where I was able to build and grow from that. All youths have the answers and are the BEST creators; "growing up" could make you lose them.

ret • ro • spect *(noun)*
   1. Look back upon (a period of time, sequence of events); remember.
   2. Contemplation of things past.

cat • a • lyst *(noun)*
   A person or event that quickly causes change or action.

Truth Through the Pen

1. What are some of your triggers?

- Dad questioning me
- Mom complaining
- Maria crying
- People moving my stuff
- When someone ditches me/flips

2. What do you think about most? (i.e. family, problems, successes)

The future and what it could be, comparing it to the past and I feel shitty. We should all prosper, I want to be a stepping stone on that journey but no one wants to join me. It's like my family doesn't care about themselves. And I always felt like they never really cared about how their actions would effect otherst, especially me.

Presta Atención

3.   What is the biggest life-changing experience you've had so far? What way have you noticed its effect on you?

Moving out, away from family & friends and having a full time job. I wanted to grow up & have choices, I got what I wanted & I feel like I was wrong. I feel it's made me serious and also feel like I failed.

4.   What are 6 rules you've created to protect yourself?

1. Do as your told.
2. Avoid conflict
3. Follow popularity
4. Alone time is key
5. Limit family time
6. Don't be like my family

5.   In this chapter I talked about creating the experiences we want. What and when was the last time you did that?

When I decided to go on a cruise alone. Everything was on my timeline, I had to get myself to California, to the boat and back. I stepped out of my comfort zone meeting new people and making memories.

6.   Life is a game, how will you win?

Be more concious of my thoughts and vocabulary. Stop when I am triggered. Bet on myself and add nuggets every day. Create the space where I can create more for myself and others

Presta Atención

Hustle & Flow

"ACTUALLY, I CAN" – INSTAGRAM MEME

Everywhere you turn, you see someone else's LIFE! On social media, riding on the bus, and my old time favorite, good ol' movies. You could be chilling and not hungry then see someone eating a slice of pizza, and all of a sudden you're hungry, and you want pizza. No matter what age you are, the fact is that your mind is never safe. We have a lot of practice doing what other people want us to do, starting with our parents. Their rules are meant to help us, but they often don't leave room for you to think for yourself. "Do this! Do that! Put that over there! No, over there!" Then if you're faced with living with one parent, neither parent, in foster care, or in an abusive home, you could be left even more scared and confused. Mostly because you feel lost without an identity, like slaves off a ship, except you don't even have a community. You feel alone and left with memories that are mostly painful which you relive until you decide you don't want to and accept what happened. At least, that was what I did.

It's not easy to understand how powerful our mind is at any age, but even worse when you're young and haven't navigated through the world for very long. Memories, experiences and challenges are meant to help you navigate through life. They should help you make better choices in the future, but a lot of times they become roadblocks instead. We react to what's happened in the past and put more focus on what we don't want. We get ourselves messed up in the game when we take this route because whatever you focus on most is EXACTLY WHAT YOU WILL GET!

As a young person, it's easy to feel powerless and react to everything that's happening around you, and you can find yourself building a defense mechanism or falling into what's socially accepted at the time. "C'mon, you know that Fetty Wop song was whack!" Or maybe you did get wrapped into his melodic rhythms, either way, finding your identity is the key.

The first thing to do is to highlight your strengths and weakness. Do not try to walk in the dark and ignore any parts of who you really are. A weakness is simply something you can work on to improve. The best thing is that there is nothing finite about who you are. Instead, you get the chance to strengthen your weaknesses. For instance, if you have a weak upper body, what would you do? You'd do some push-ups, lift some weights, whatever you have to do, right? You have to focus on the area until you get the results you want. A weakness won't go away if you ignore it, and sometimes, like a person with skinny legs wearing shorts, it will stick out even more. Look at your weaknesses and WORK THEM OUT. It's pretty easy to ignore what you aren't great at, but the longer I waited to work on a weakness, I noticed the worse it got.

For many years I didn't acknowledge how much being upset with my mother affected my romantic relationships. Weaknesses show up in many different ways, and it's not all about being a bad reader or being horrible at math. There were choices I was making on a daily basis that I wasn't even aware of. Though there are many technologies that can get you around math and reading, what I couldn't get around was self-sabotage. I had become an expert at unconsciously self-sab-otaging by reacting from a place of pain and disappointment.

When I started dating and engaging in romantic relationships, I never gave them a real chance. Once I would have an expe-rience with someone, I would move on. I wouldn't call, re-spond, or want anything to do with them anymore. It was like a switch flipped. The thought of the person wanting to be with me or actually liking me never crossed my mind, and when it did, it scared me more than anything.

I started to realize I had abandonment issues. I was actually scared the other person would leave me. My mother did. It took me most of my 20's and even some of my 30's to let go of this pain and strengthen my weakness: my mind. Our thoughts manifest in our world. When I strengthened my mind, I strengthened my actions.

self-sab • o • tage *(noun)*
  The conscious or unconscious obstruction of or damage to
  any cause, movement, activity, effort, etc.

Your strengths come in handy when you're talking about weaknesses. Strengths not only make you shine, stand out, and be confident: they also help in strengthening and fixing weaknesses. One of my strengths now is having a positive mind. I had to work really hard at this since I wasn't always able to strengthen a weakness. When I decided I wanted bet-ter and that I wanted to find love, I was able to do the work. Some people believe knowing what you don't want is key, but I've found that knowing what I wanted brought better results.

When I focused on what I did want, more support toward that thing popped up. If I focused on what I didn't want, more of that popped up, along with more reasons why I don't want it! This was incredibly stressful but then I started to realize an easy way to focus on what you want is by setting goals. Goals birthed in positivity won't fall victim to adversity. They will push you through all the obstacles and help you hustle!

My Life

When I first became a dancer and became a part of the dance community in NYC, I was like Kanye. I yelled about all the things I thought the community lacked, how everyone was doing the same thing, and praising myself for being different. I met this break-dancer named Midnight and he and I would work on choreography for hours. He would teach me how to pop and I would work with him on choreography.

For years, although they may have respected my work, many people couldn't stand my arrogance and because of that, I didn't go far. I taught and did stage shows and did cool stuff but I was always looking at all the others going on tour and getting real recognition. To be honest, I didn't believe I deserved it and I sure wasn't working hard enough for it. I didn't realize that, once again, I was doing things that would bring me the opposite of what I actually wanted.

How can you be a part of a community if all you do is bash it? How can you expect to go far if nobody likes you? I became a bit of a recluse and popped up every once in a while until I had a vision and left NYC altogether. I left because I felt stuck. No one ran me out, there was no revolt against Octavia, but Octavia needed new space to grow.

I left to Atlanta and then to Miami where I created a whole new mindset. I knew what I wanted to happen, so I came up with a mindset that was aligned with actions that would take me further than I ever thought! I stopped pushing people away and praised them more instead. I made it a rule to do what I said I was going to do. No matter how challenging it was, I would push through it. I have never WORKED so hard in my life.... But DAMMMMMNNNNN, it's paying off! If I left NYC doing the same thing or thinking the same way, I would not be thriving like I am now, period.

<3 <3 <3

It's important to know that it won't always be easy, but it won't always be hard either. If you accept that what comes to you is what's meant for you, you will continue to attract more of what you want and need. This is what we call a "flow." Knowing what you want creates a "flow" in your life. You don't need to know exactly how you will get it, just that you want it and if it's meant for you it will come. Some will think it's luck but it's really you connecting with your true purpose. And when that happens, it takes you closer to whatever God you believe in to create some real magic!

Get It!

Be sure to give thanks for everything! Be thankful for every challenge and every opportunity. You may know what you want, but the way you will get it is laced with the unknown. Pay attention, you have to hustle to get the flow.

Truth Through the Pen

1.   Who are you? When answering this, use adjectives to describe yourself. Keep listing these adjectives until you feel finished.

Patient, Honest, Trustworthy, Loyal, Hard Working, Beautiful, Cute, Funny, Goofy, Soft, Caring, Sweet, To the point, Open Minded, Curious, Spontaneous, Supportive, Smart, Arrogant, Rude, Snippy, Inconciderate, Condescending, Bully

2.   What are your strengths? List 6 and choose ONE to share how you utilize and benefit from it.

1. Relaxed 2. Logical 3. Dedicated
4. "I can" mentality 5. Always seeking info
6. Passionated.
4. I can go from sleeping all day to a full time 9-5. This helps me acquire new challenges and see them through to the end. Workout challenges, punctuality, Biting the bullet when no one else wants to or is able to.

3.   What are your weaknesses? List 6 and choose ONE to share how it shows up in your everyday life.

Lazy, procrastinator, inconsistent, accomodating for others, ignorance, easily distracted

4.   What do you want most out of this life?

I want to see everyone around me succeed in life, with money never being an issue I want to be able to pick up and go somewhere with my loved ones whenever I feel like. To do what I want, when I want

5.   How are you going for what you want?

Developing habits that will put me in a better position to receive opportunities
- Exercise   - maintain healthy relations
- Self care /Vacation   - establish routine
- Reading / Education   - Reflection

6.   Life is a flow, will you be a rolling ocean or a still river?

I want to be a rolling ocean, I want to be someone people can count on but for greater things than emotional support. I want to create opportunities for others.

#TeamCarry-On

THESE MOUNTAINS THAT YOU ARE CARRYING,

YOU WERE ONLY SUPPOSED TO CLIMB THEM –
INSTAGRAM MEME

When you take a flight somewhere you have a choice to carry-on or check in your luggage. A bag that's checked in will likely cost you extra money but you can take a lot more things with you. A carry-on is usually free but really limits the amount of things you can bring with you.

My Life

I called my mother when I was 13 and I told her that I forgive her. I was always blaming her for the hell I was experiencing here on earth. I told her I needed to forgive her because I wasn't about to let her be the reason I went to hell for real! I finally felt free.

<3 <3 <3

I really felt freer and the gesture really empowered me to move forward with my life. I took the power back, but I wouldn't realize I didn't really forgive her until almost 18 years later. That's nuts!

This is a really hard chapter.

It's hard because forgiveness and acceptance are the hardest things to do when you're in pain or have been hurt by someone who claims that they love you. You learn quickly that disappointment and pain are fixtures in the human experience like love and joy. The issue is, within our dysfunctional family lives, we aren't taught how to handle any of it. When I was upset about something, my foster mother would often say, "you'll get it over it." I hated that because it was so dismissive and void of any concern about my feelings. Although my foster mother and I had a great relationship, she had no idea the damage she was doing. Most of what we learn is through example and usually from a warped perception.

per • cep • tion *(noun)*
  A way of regarding, understanding, or interpreting something; a mental impression.

warped *(verb)*
  To become or cause to become bent or twisted out of shape.

Put simply in the book "A Course In Miracles":

*"The Golden Rule asks you to do unto others as you would have them do unto you. **This means that the perception of both must be accurate.** The Golden Rule is for appropriate behavior. You cannot behave appropriately unless you perceive correctly."*

We make our own rules of what's right and wrong, rarely consulting the other person. We rarely consider what they've been through or what they have going on. I also realized that even treating someone like you want to be treated can be a recipe for disaster because you are NOT the same person. Perhaps taking the time to see how they want to be treated is a better solution.

Either way, I wasted a lot of time being upset with my mother. I thought I was in pain because of what she did, but really I was in pain because I couldn't let it go. I just couldn't accept her not wanting to be a mom. I couldn't accept that maybe her bringing me into this world was her only purpose in my life. That alone, I've realized, was the best thing she could ever given me and humanity. Along with all those pills, I also had to swallow that that she could only do what she was capable of. She too had her own path and purpose in this world that didn't include ME.

That's A Lot!

But it's a must. When I started to piece all these truths to-gether, I began to stop blaming myself. That was major and really something that was in my subconscious. I slowly began to let go of thinking that I wasn't good enough and realized that it had nothing to do with me. My mother battled drug addiction and admitted to using drugs while she was pregnant with me, while she's been clean for a very long time, her pain and her demons haven't gone away. One of which could be that she just does not have an interest in being a mother the same way that I have no interest in being a construction worker.

It's human nature to take things personally. We came into this world wanting and needing to be fed, changed, and held. If it didn't happen quickly enough, we cried. As we get older, we are taught to do things on our own and we feel good about our independence, but we still have the tendency to cry if something doesn't go our way. This isn't actually the worst part, or the part that is the most hindering to our development, which is being unaware of our ability to take responsibility for our life experiences. We are the creators of our world. We quickly go from needing to be changed to forming opinions and thoughts. Decision and choice are ours whether we realize it or not.

I remember seeing a boy in school who would talk back to the teacher, and friends who would demand their parents for nice toys or specific foods they wanted. I would look at them in awe, thinking to myself "I can't believe they said that!" I was always shocked that they had the courage to do that. They hadn't let themselves be bound by the rules that I did. Right or wrong, they were exercising their human right to decide what they wanted and made a choice to say it. That was something I myself never felt comfortable doing.

The teacher threatened the little boy to go to the principal's office and to call his home, to which he would shrug carelessly and reply "I don't care!" WHAT?! It was so exciting to me! I knew he was in the wrong, but I also respected him so much! He took ownership and responsibility for his actions, projected that to the teacher, and rendered her powerless. Adults always seem to have the power but here he is, this 9-year-old boy, taking it all! He probably did get a beating when he got home, probably got suspended too, but he took responsibility for it, he owned it. He wasn't a victim, he was a creator!

proj • ect *(verb)*
> To throw or cause to move forward or outward. Extend outward beyond something else.

Acceptance is the key to forgiveness but impossible to get if you don't take responsibility for the part you play in your life, which is the lead role! I was done being a victim of circumstance.

Victims NEVER WIN.

Victims are only that. The one who is blamed will always have all the power. Do we know the victims of the "Son of Sam" or any other murderer? NO, we only know the murderer. The accused is rarely around to help you pick up the pieces. After all, why would they stick around for that? Acceptance helped me help myself and to help others down the line. Year after year "right" and "wrong" became more and more irrelevant.

ir • rel • e • vant *(adjective)*
   Unimportant, useless.

When I look back on my life, I realize that if anything, I mean ANYTHING, were different, I wouldn't be where I am right now. I could have children, I could be super lost, and I would not have met half the amazing people I have in my life! I needed it all to happen this way. How much insight could I give in this book if my parents raised me, and in the way I saw fit? How much could I relate to you if I didn't experience a drug abusing mother AND Catholic schooling?

in • sight *(noun)*
   The ability to have clear and deep understanding of a complicated situation.

Acceptance gives you the key to unlock the door to the place you're trapped. Unlocking that door sets you free to move forward, and moving forward gives you strength. With that strength you can flex your muscles of forgiveness. It's almost effortless! Okay, granted you will have to put forward a lot of effort, but it will get easier. People always say, "I can forgive but I won't forget." This saying is exactly why people stay mad. It's redundant and usually said from a place of hurt and fear.

Forgiveness has nothing to do with the other person, nor does it need to start with them. Forgiveness starts with yourself; forgiving yourself for the part that you played. "I won't forget" right, because pain, like joy, leaves an imprint on your spirit. You won't forget because you don't want to make the same mistake twice, even though you might! Forgiveness is not for the other person, it's for you!

re • dun • dant *(adjective)*
A thing or action that is unnecessary or could be left out.

My Life

In February 1995, my sister, myself, and my grandmother went to the foster care agency (what we affectionately referred to as "The Agency") for a routine check-in or review. These visits were just conversations with our social worker about what was happening in our world. I used to be a pretty quiet young kid. My grandmother was always strict with very clear "adult" and "child" lines distinguished. We didn't joke with each other and affection between us didn't exist. My grandmother was a disciplinarian first, and a provider second. There weren't kisses, hugs or sweet words. My sister did sneak in her bed when she had bad dreams and although I never considered doing so, I was still jealous of that. I probably could have if I had tried but I never wanted to risk getting in trouble. My grandmother had a history of being hurt and let down, and the decision I was about to make at the agency meant my days of living with her would soon be over, just like I wanted.

When I got in the meeting room with my social worker and she asked how things were I began to say all the things I knew

41

would get me taken away. I told her that I didn't want to live with my grandmother anymore and that she hit us. Laws were changing at this point and parents were losing power. They were no longer able to beat their children. Although I told the agency she gave us beatings, the fact is my grandmother was not in any way abusive, and was a single parent to us. They took us from her that day. We didn't even go back to the house. We never said goodbye.

I imagine that the train ride from Brooklyn to Far Rockaway was one of the most painful my grandmother ever took.

<3 <3 <3

It would take me a month before I could get up the courage to call and speak to my grandmother. It would take me nearly a year before I could speak to her without crying from all the guilt I felt. It would take nearly 20 years before I would forgive myself for the way I treated her and betrayed her. The truth is, my grandmother is still the greatest, strongest, most caring, loving and loyal person I have ever met in my life. She sacrificed her life for her family. When she passed away in a nursing home, I think my mother was by her side. I'm glad she had that. She is still very close to me and is one of the reasons I'm writing this book. Her transcendence from earth was an upgrade to my life, and humanity.

tran • scend *(verb)*
  Be or go beyond the range or limits. Surpass go beyond, rise above.

"I WHIPPED MY OWN BACK AND ASKED FOR DOMINION AT YOUR FEET." – BEYONCÉ

I've accepted the situation as part of my story, and although it took me 20 years, I did finally forgive myself and find closure. Nothing happens overnight or even years sometimes, but doing little by little everyday helps you get there. I started off accepting small things that would upset me, like missing the bus that would get me to school or work on time. Then I moved on to bigger things like how to cope when someone hurt my feelings. Instead of getting upset, I would take responsibility, telling myself "I could have gotten up earlier and left on time to catch my bus." or "I knew they weren't that into me, they showed me that by being unresponsive to my texts and calls." Often times I realized I didn't accept things because I was in denial about it and always talking myself out of the truth. Nowadays, I make it practice to keep it real with myself.

There's a saying about giving other people the "benefit of the doubt." I've tried this and in most situations the outcome was a fail! Why? Because your "doubt" in these situations is actually your gut, also known as your intuition. Your intuition is really messages coming straight from the creator. It's loud to our bodies and low to our minds, which is why we don't listen to it as much as we should. We mostly react to what our minds say, but if we listened to our intuition on the same level that we felt it, we'd make better choices and have better flow in our lives.

After you've accepted situations as they are, and after you've forgiven yourself and whoever else you choose to forgive, the door you've opened to free yourself can now be closed behind you. Now that I think about it, that's probably why it's called "closure." Closure often times keeps you from walking back to where you've come from. Closure often requires more steps than acceptance and forgiveness. A conversation with a person, a visit to a place, a removal or addition of a thing - or all of the above! You won't know what you need for closure until you take that trippy trip through acceptance and forgiveness.

clo • sure *(noun)*
A feeling that an emotional or traumatic experience has been resolved.

> *"NEW BEGINNINGS ARE OFTEN DISGUISED AS PAINFUL ENDINGS" – LAO TZU*

The start line and the finish line are usually the same and often look the same. It's the feeling that you have once you get there that makes difference. Letting go of those things was the best thing I did for myself. We carry so much of the past with us on a daily basis. We never realize the sweat beads forming on our spirit. Never noticing the walls built are blocking the limitless good that could be coming our way. Never paying attention to how sore our efforts have become, losing impact each time. Never realizing that we're over stretching and losing the elasticity of our future way before we've even gotten there. We're tired and worn out before we've been able to do what we are here to do! The sooner you take the trip, the better. You'll get to your destination. Just pack light for this journey. Keep calm and carry on with your carry-on!

Truth Through the Pen

1.   Who are the top 3 people you feel you have to forgive and why? (Hint: You should be one of them.)

Myself, my mom, my sister.
Myself for being selfish at times when I should
have been paying attention to the situation.
My mom for behaving in only the way she knows how.
My sister for just trying to live her best life

2.   What are 3 situations you've found hard to accept and why?

1. Feeling the need to separate from my family,
they should be helping me but maybe I don't accept it
2. I don't want a regular job but no one else
wants to help me build something. I might lose everyone if
I do.
3. Following trends or social. Maybe I feel like I'll
never have attention like that, but I might not want it.

3.   'What was the worst thing that has happened in your life? How has it helped you?

The entire struggle it took for me to move
out. From my moms to my dads to my

how THE hell did YOU do THAT?!

sisters then to my boyfriends, then back with
my dad and mom to finally being alone.
Now I know it's something I can do
again.

4.   When or what makes you feel powerful?

- When I have a group of people laughing at
something I said.
- Reading & learning new ideas
- Exercise
- A finished to do list

5.   What was the last situation you found closure in?

Fighting with Maurice. We laid out
our feelings and it made me realize I
also have a lot of work to do on myself.
I can't expect from him what I won't do.

6. Life can be a long journey, how have you lightened your load lately?

Yes, 2 vacations back to back has put me in reset mode. Setting boundaries with my parents and not speaking to my sister has given me a lot of space to breathe think, & work.

CREME DE LA CHROME

"IT'S LIKE THE FAMILY YOU CAN CHOOSE."-
HARRISON COLE, 14 YRS. OLD

My Life

So much of my youth was focused on family and the fact that I didn't have a traditional one I could call my own. It was like everyone but me knew their mom, dad, aunts, and uncles. What could people my age do for me? I used to be bullied as a kid and didn't connect with or trust my peers. I never felt lonely though, because I learned subconsciously from my family life that people came and went, so I had fun where I could and I didn't get very attached. Friends weren't what I wanted to attach myself to. I wanted a family. When I went into foster care I made a vow to myself that I would never be bullied again. Along with that vow came cutting people off at the drop of a dime. I had a social, funny, loud personality. Getting kicked out of home after home kept me from making stable friends, but it helped me to be interchangeable in different places. When I finally found a stable home, I learned quickly how having friends really influences your thoughts and actions.

I remember my first real friend. Her name was Beverly. We both grew up with our grandmothers so we connected over that. She was also strong and didn't bite her tongue and would pop off if she needed to. I felt safe around her. She was an Aries, always kept it real, and was a really giving person. I would come over and she would make us sandwiches and we'd ride our bikes around for hours. I remember two days with her so vividly.

Beverly and I were like frick and frack, always together, always riding our bikes. We were opposites as much as we were alike. I was pretty "square" compared to her bold personality. One day we were riding our bikes past a fruit stand and she stuck her hand and nabbed something. I did the same right after! I remember feeling filled with excitement and a little fear and a tad guilty but I enjoyed that mango. Our adventures went from stealing fruit on bike rides to cutting school! As my luck would have it, we got caught! Her grandmother was on the same bus we took to the train station to go into Manhattan. She saw Beverly and yelled her name and the rest of us ran for our lives!

We decided to cut school that morning, so we didn't really have a plan but we continued into the city. We went to the Brooklyn Bridge area where the World Trade Center was and ended up stranded there. We hopped the trains, all the while scared, and got back to Queens thanks to the sympathy of the bus driver.

We got back way too early to be back from school so we broke into an abandoned house and spent time together until it was finally time to go back home. My foster mom asked if I had homework and I said I had done it already. It was nearly 8:30pm and I felt so in the clear! I was upstairs getting ready for bed (on the third floor of the house) when I hear my foster father call out my name... *Gulp* I tried to keep my cool.... I WAS BUSTED! Beverly's grandmother called to tell them what we did and I was grounded! I was in either 7th or 8th grade and I never cut school again!

Fear Is One Hell of An Organic Drug!

Our friendship faded gradually after that, mostly because she moved but I also began to make new friends; ever since then I've made a slew of friends, most of whom have opened my mind so much and showed me what it was truly like to be a part of a community. They protected me, they shared with me, they taught me things, they exposed me to life, they under-stood me, they accepted me, they enjoyed me, I enjoyed them, they loved me and... I loved them.

Friends began to show me how I deserved to be treated. They didn't misuse me and while I was protective of myself and wouldn't have allowed it, I'm glad I didn't have to. They were my safe haven. They were my diary. I would, of course, like to take full credit for all that I am, all that I can be and will be, but I can't.

While growing up, I wasn't exposed to travel in the way that I know it now, which is frequent and extensive. Travel has been a very special catalyst for a lot of my growth, even though I had no desire for it while growing up. When I lived with my foster parents, we'd take a road trip to Atlanta or Maryland to see my foster father's family, but that was the extent of it. Traveling abroad wasn't even something in the conversation and neither were any foods outside of the Black/Caribbean culture. I was pretty sheltered as a young girl; both my grandmother and my foster parents ran a tight ship. Yes, you can have natural desires to see the world or different things, but for me it never came up. Friends of all kinds were the ones that opened my mind to a lot of things. All I used to think about was being able to support myself, thanks to my foster father. I also thought about being happy and how credit cards are bad. My friends talked about things I never thought about or even considered, like college, about holding onto virginity until marriage, and about religion, music, ideas, and the future.

viv • id • ly (adverb):
   Something done in a clear, graphic or very detailed way.

ex • ten • sive *(adjective)*
   Large in amount or scale. Covering or affecting a large area.

"HOW CAN YOU MISS SOMETHING YOU'VE NEVER HAD" – SOMEBODY BEFORE ME

By the time I was in my senior year of high school, my relationship with my new foster parents was dead. I barely talked to them and they didn't respect me at all. They pushed me to apply for college, yet they never helped me with the process. I was in and out of the agency asking questions that no one seemed to know. I spent a lot of time looking for something or someone who could give me a clue. I eventually found out how to submit my college applications for free since I was a foster child. I learned how to apply for TAP and PELL to get money for school too.

Since I was in foster care, I was entitled to a free education, a benefit of not having a family! I got letters of recommendation from teachers and though I never thought I'd actually get into college, it was active and fun trying. I really wanted to escape being in a home.

I began to get letters back and was accepted to Lincoln University, a historically black college. St. John's University also accepted me under some pretense of primary classes to boost my GPA. It was a no brainer, LINCOLN HERE I COME!!! When I got to the bottom of reading my acceptance letter; however, I saw that there was a holding fee I had to pay by a certain time and I DID NOT HAVE IT.

At the time, I was working at the office of the mayor through a cooperative program I was accepted into. I got to work there for two weeks out of the month and go to school for two weeks as a way a way to prepare me for the working world. Funny part is, the offices were right across the street from the Brooklyn Bridge where I was stranded while cutting school years before!

Anyway, I couldn't afford it and mentioned it in passing to a coworker, who was an older woman. She believed in me and gave me the money to send to the school with just enough time. A couple of weeks had gone by, I had spoken to my soon to be roommate and I was feeling great! I then got the bill from college and saw that there was a lot of money that was not accounted for, so I called them. Being a foster child was supposed to help me get free shit, right? They explained to me that because I was a foster child in New York City, college benefits would only work for me there. FML, I'm stuck! Do I take out loans? UGH! I DIDN'T EVEN WANT TO GO TO COLLEGE IN THE FIRST PLACE! Now I'm going accumulate debt just to do it?! Just days before I was meant to touchdown on campus, I called admissions to discharge myself. I remember the day so vividly.

I sat outside of the McDonalds I worked at. I was CRUSHED. Devastated mostly because I no longer had an escape from this home. This whole time my foster parents never even asked me how things were going, what was happening, nothing. It seemed like their only concern was how soon I'd be leaving. They never provided me with money or moral support. I felt so defeated.

When I got home that night from work, they were sitting on the steps outside.

"I had to discharge myself, I couldn't afford to go," I told them. With a blank stare, they responded, "Okay." — I went to my room and balled my eyes out. No one asked how I planned to move forward, or how I was actually going succeed at life. Then I get a call from my friend saying she's near my place. She lived all the way on the other side of town and drove to me to just to sit, talk and comfort me without me asking.

I've always been very strong but I was at the lowest point in my life at the time. I envisioned putting a gun to my head while home alone on New Year's Eve. I kept asking myself "what am I even here for?" I felt so trapped and powerless, but my friends were there for me the whole way through. I'm glad I didn't end my life then, even though I would contemplate it again as an adult and understand it on a totally different level.

how THE hell did YOU do THAT?!

"THE GRASS GETS GREENER BUT YOU CAN'T SEE THE OTHER SIDE"- OLAMIDE FAISON

For many people, as they get older they maintain a certain group of friends. For others, close friends become the foundation, and like the foundation of a skyscraper building, you begin to rarely see them. As a youngster, I'd pride myself on "not having many friends" or "keeping my circle tight." Letting go of that rule allowed me to meet more people. While I can never forget the importance of childhood friends, being open to making new friends changed the game. I met friends that would connect me with the "right people" that would advance my career (or give me a job in general), friends that I collaborated with artistically, and friends that exposed me to fine foods and international travel.

One day I was at a NYE hotel party with my friend, NYCole. I met her because her manager at the time had also managed a group I was working with and wanted me to work with her too. She was a dancer and a recording artist, who was also an Aries and who I would collaborate with for the next 10 years, but who knew!

The ball drops and everyone goes back to chatting, when this girl comes up to me and asks, "So.... what's your story?" I'm tripped up because no one has ever asked me something like that so bluntly, especially not a stranger. "Do you really wanna know? It's a long one," I said. I give her a bit of my story, she's taken and from then on, we become great friends. I began to hang out with her and her friends all the time at her penthouse in Union Square. I had never been in a penthouse before that. In fact, it took me a while to figure out that the "PH" in her apt number meant "Penthouse".

My friend Lauren and her crew had been friends for about ten years, they were all EXTREMELY smart, quick witted, used big words that I never heard before, and smoked weed often. I loved that they never cared that I passed on the rotation or that I asked what the words they were using meant whenever I couldn't put it together contextually myself. Google wasn't around back then! They were a bit bougie and knew all the top promoters. While they were regulars at the most official parties, they also weren't too flashy or materialistic. They knew a lot but didn't feel like they had to prove anything. Even thinking and writing about them is making me feel more poetic!

Lauren calls me up one day and asks me if I want to go to Puerto Rico. I was 23, had never been out of the country, and never thought to, but I said SURE! She told me she had a travel agent and would front it and I give her the money back before we go. This is after two weeks of knowing her! Two weeks later, we were on the plane! She, like Niccole and Beverly, was an Aries too. At different points in my life they all taught me a lot about being free, being open minded, adventurous, being fearless, and thinking about the future.

Growing up in the system, even though I had solid foster parents, no one was really talking to me about the future. My friends were the only inspirational fixtures in my life. They inspired me to keep making goals and having aspirations. These three ladies in particular. I never thought to travel before I met Lauren.

how THE hell did YOU do THAT?!

The healthy, loving, and caring vibes of great friends made me enthusiastic about experiencing new people, places, and things. I also met many people through the people I knew. By the end of the year I met Lauren, I met a director through one of her friends and wound up in a musical that premiered in Barbados, which meant I needed a passport.

<3 <3 <3

There have been droves of people who have helped me heal, learn, and advance throughout my life. They all came in the form of friends and unspoken mentors. My life would LITER-ALLY be nothing if it weren't for my friends. In this category I am also referencing adults who befriended me and became an ear and confidant when I didn't have a voice, like my foster mother's best friend, Allison. She was my first mentor. She was the first adult not caught up in being an adult and who saw me, heard me even when I didn't say anything, and listened. She also never chose sides when telling me how to deal with parents and people. Allison made me feel safe and her friend-ship made me feel like I had someone on my side. Me choosing to open up to her and her making herself available when I needed her made life better. Allison felt like a friend, not an adult with power over me. I respected her deeply and she re-spected me.

droves *(noun)*
  A large number of people or things doing or undergoing the same thing.

con • fi • dant *(noun)*
  A person with whom one shares a secret or private matter, trusting them not to repeat it to others.

CRÈME DE LA CHROME

men • tor *(noun)*
   Someone who teaches or gives help and advice to a less experienced and often younger person.

con • tex • u • al(ly) (adverb):
   Defining a word based on the words or phrases surrounding
   it.

fix • ture *(noun)*
   Something securely, and usually permanently attached. A
   person or thing that is established in a particular place or
   situation.

*"PEOPLE WHO WANT THE BEST FOR YOU IS
WHAT'S BEST FOR YOU." – SOMEONE'S
INSTAGRAM MEME*

Our life experiences can cause us to block our blessings. We
think we're protecting ourselves, but we don't realize that
when we build a wall we don't only keep others away, but we
keep ourselves from others. We hinder our ability to grow and
learn past the space we are in. We stay so immersed in that
space that we only draw in others that are just like us, stuck
with the same pain, and same blocks- both of y'all are stuck.

When you do go out into the world, which you can't avoid, you
will cause more hurt to yourself and others. Everyone has their
own path and each moment along that path you are building.
We all have this ability. We are creators, but we cannot create
in a beneficial way alone. When you keep your thoughts clear,
remember what you want and create goals with the betterment of the whole in mind. With that approach, you will get

better and better at choosing whom you want to help build your path.

Being an open and giving person may lead you to disappointments, but as a human, a refrigerator, or a pot on the stove, you have to be open to give and receive. This is where things get tricky. It's when you have to be really ONE with yourself, and most of all, exclusive about the people you choose to invest in. NOT IN A SUPERFICIAL WAY, but you are a prized person. All good financial investments have a return. That's also true for every life investment and experience, but it always comes in the form of a lesson.

Once I learned to pay close attention to my life lessons, I was able to take quick action. It's easy to assume that things just happen to us, but that's not true. We play a part in everything that happens in life. Life is like a game, if you don't learn the lesson (or beat the level) you will experience (or do the level over) again and again and again.

Most of the time it will be painful and you will make mistakes and get annoyed with yourself because you are the one allowing it. That is, until you learn to let go of the investments that bring you down or don't have the type of returns that benefit you. Instead of giving a situation the "benefit of the doubt," listen to your gut, your intuition, and your spirit. Why give the benefit to something your body and spirit are already showing you is not for you? I've never received any benefit from doubting. Learning to listen to yourself is a powerful choosing tool.

Selfishness Gets a Bad Rap.

The best friends make efforts to make your world better without self-gains. The great ones bring harmony, peace, love, and

CRÈME DE LA CHROME

an abundance of amazing experiences. Choose the "Crème De La Crème!" Then watch life for you and them take flight to new heights!

crème de la crème *(noun)*
  The very best. The best of the best.

The people you surround yourself with are mirror reflections of you, like looking into a piece of chrome. How you see yourself will be the defining factor in what people you keep around you. Everything comes back to you as a result of your conscious and subconscious mind (action or reaction).

Actions are made with thought. Example: You go to take something out of the oven and get a hand mitt to take it out.

Reactions are done without thought. Example: You touch something you didn't know was hot and immediately pull your hand back fast.

I wanted to make choosing my friends an intentional action, something I did consciously. I remember being shocked when I found out Leonardo DiCaprio and Tobey Maguire were best friends. I wondered how Jay-Z and the dude from Coldplay became friends. Many genuine friends appear to be "odd couples" but they help each other grow. That exchange is important in all relationships but since you are often with friends more than you are with your family, it's even more important.

Just like the evil queen, the mirror will only show you the truth. She asked who was the fairest of them all and the mirror said, NOT YOU!

how THE hell did YOU do THAT?!

Truth Through the Pen

1.   What part do friends play in your life? (Important, not that serious, like family, or just entertainment?)

More like family than my own
blood.

2.   How do you define a "friend?"

Someone I can trust

3.   How do you help your friends become better? Are you the BEST friend you could be to all of them? (Give as many examples as you can think of.)

I thought I was the best friend there is to have. Now though observing, I see I try to bring new ideas to the table or say what others won't or are too afraid to say. I haven't created boundaries and this hurts me rather than help my friends.

4.   Have your long-term friends helped you become better? If yes, how? If not, why do you feel that way?

Yes. A handful of friends are so diverse in terms of knowledge, age, experiences, and social groups. Deej, CJ, Brian, the girls. Everyone has opened my mind in some aspect, whether its showing me what it's like to run a business, what a real LIFE looks like, or just to have fun. I am who I am because of who I choose to influence me.

5.   Who was the last friend to actively help you achieve a goal? (It can be anything from work, school, or a concert you wanted to attend.)

The babies all come together to make sure we had an awesome time in Canmore.

6.   Life is about who you know. The better you know yourself, the better you'll be able to choose. What reflection of yourself did you pick from today?

Deej, CJ & Brian because they have been around for a certain length of time and in that time I have never felt that they've steered me wrong

CRÈME DE LA CHROME

~~Passport &~~
~~Borderlines~~

"EVERY NEXT LEVEL OF YOUR LIFE WILL DEMAND A DIFFERENT VERSION OF YOU" – UNKNOWN

People cross the line every damn day, why shouldn't you!? Why should I stay in the same hood, or do the same things as others? Where do I expect to get by doing that? The best thing foster care did for me was keep me on the move so I could stay on my toes.

My Life

When I was 14 years old I told my foster parents I wanted a job. My friends and I had all gotten our working papers from school and were ready to make our own money. I didn't get an allowance and I couldn't just get money if I asked. They didn't take me shopping very often and I wasn't someone's favorite who got gifts and nice things. I barely got things I liked for Christmas and I always had to wear my sneakers until the heels fell off before we went to the flea market to get new old ones. I never complained but I just wanted to make money to have the freedom to buy what I wanted and what I liked since they wouldn't.

Passport & Borderlines

I don't know where my foster mother was on this day but I vividly remember having this conversation with my foster father who worked a lot and was the proverbial enforcer type. She might have been there but letting him handle it. Either way, he sat on the bed, half watching TV and half talking to me, and asked me "why do you want a job?" I wanted to scream "because ya'll do the bare minimum for me and have very little care about what I like so I want to do it my damn self!" But I didn't have the balls, so I simply responded "so I can afford to get things for myself." Predictably, he said, "you don't need to have a job. All you need to do is focus on school." I WAS PISSED! Even though his answer did not surprise me, it still annoyed the hell out of me. Why wouldn't they let me do for myself what they wouldn't do for me!?

I might have just sighed, but my insides were on fire. I hated having no real power over my life. As I walked down the stairs in anger, he said calmly, "you don't need to focus on money, only focus on your happiness." It was super genuine and though I cared NOT about his philosophical moment, it penetrated all the way to my spirit and never left. I have subscribed to that line and still embrace it as my philosophy. It's funny how life works sometimes. I am really grateful I wasn't so caught up in my feelings that I didn't listen to what he said. I was able to digest his words. Sometimes when you're angry, your wires get crossed and you miss the lesson. Using my foster father's words as a philosophy helped me make a lot of decisions that have pushed me forward and towards the right people.

pro • ver • bi • al *(adjective)*
   Well known, especially so as to be stereotypical.

in • tu • i • tive *(adjective)*

Having the ability to know or understand things without any proof or evidence.

i • de • ol • o • gy:
The ideas and manner of thinking characteristic of a group, social class, or individual.

phi • los • o • phy *(noun)*
A theory or attitude held by a person or organization that acts as guiding principles for behavior.

Take what you need and throw the rest away.

As a youngster, I heard millions of statements that left me feeling muted and powerless. "Speak when you're spoken to," "stay in a child's place," What type of person did they think they would make with ideologies like that? I followed their shitty rules but thankfully it taught me the art of listening. What I gained from not having the freedom to speak when I wanted to was the ability to understand, read people, think, be curious, write, create art, and feel EVERYTHING.

Being able to identify when someone was happy, angry, annoyed, pensive, etc. turned out to be a useful tool because it helped me navigate and strengthen my already intuitive nature. Listening helped me become better in the ways that those around me lacked, and gauge if someone was genuine or not. My ability to feel was tough because I felt so much all the time. But when you do anything "all the time" you become a master at it. Although there were moments where I felt powerless, I did not adopt powerlessness as a personal quality. I used what worked for me from past experiences to expand myself. I didn't know what I was doing at the time, but I knew

Passport & Borderlines

I wanted to be better and do better. The more I did, the more people paid attention and gained interest. That felt amazing, but I never let people get too close.

For years, people I spent substantial time with didn't even know my last name, and no one thought to ask. I would know everything about them, their family history and more, yet they wouldn't even know my last name. I would share with them just enough for both of us to feel taken care of. This brought a lot of people into my life, along with a collection of experiences.

Most of the friends I grew up with in Queens never left. Being open enough to connect with people led me to different parts of NYC. I was in Manhattan, the Bronx, Brooklyn, Staten Island, and even made it to Puerto Rico and Barbados! Traveling CHANGED THE GAME! My vocabulary expanded, I had friends from NYC to Michigan to California. My taste in food, music, thoughts, and dress all shifted dramatically year after year. My general interests shifted too.

Every place you go has its own energy and way of doing things. Learning those things sharpened my mind, expanded my thought process and even how I thought things are meant to be done. It all took me to another level in this game of life. It's crazy, it even made me better at things I was already good at, like dance.

My friends had been working for years at this point, but I ended up leaving my foster parents home at 16 and going back into the system. When I did, the first order of business was getting myself a job. I got TWO! One was at the McDonald's that some of my friends worked at in Forest Hills, in a white neighborhood that was far from where I was from. They didn't hire me at first, but I came around often and applied again a year later and got the job. My job there is where I learned to speak Spanish. Even though my biological family is from Panama, a Spanish Speaking country in Central America with a strong Afro-Caribbean presence, my grandmother never taught us. I always wanted to learn and felt very connected to the Spanish culture. She would speak it and I would be in awe. So when I got this job where 95% of my co-workers spoke Spanish, I began asking how to say specific words, then sentences, and then began to notice the relationships and take stabs at it on my own.

My accent is flawless and I now speak a pretty decent amount considering I'm self-taught. But if I never ventured out of the town I grew up in then I wouldn't have learned much. Things got even more intense when I got older and left the country to truly experience different cultures.

You can only give from the overflow.

There are times where you feel like you have nothing else to give; a time where you feel you've given so much and not much has been given back. It's not about doing something to get something in return, it's about the flow or cycle of energy exchange that life is all about. If it doesn't rain, the well runs dry. Dry because although it didn't rain, the well still provided. I was a dry well in 2013. I felt completely depleted. I felt tired and uninspired and like I needed to be selfish.

de • ple • ted *(verb)*
   To decrease seriously or exhaust the abundance or supply of.

Selfishness gets such a bad rap.

Passport & Borderlines

How are you going to be useful to anyone if you feel like crap and don't have what you need? I decided I needed more experiences and wanted to go to places where I would be both needed and appreciated. I just finished reading a book called "Be Here Now" by Ram Dass. In the book, he talked about his travels to India. India and Tibet were places I wanted to visit after watching a documentary called "Shortcut To Nirvana." The year before, when a friend brought up the subject of going, I said sure, even though I had no idea how I could afford such an expensive trip. Ram Dass had money because he was a Harvard professor.

Over that summer, a lot of changes were happening. My nieces and nephew were now in foster care. When I found out that I couldn't afford to take them, I was completely heartbroken. I also began a new contract job that summer and it was a nightmare. The book "Be Here Now" became a refuge for me. To me, it symbolized freedom, exploration, and spiritual elevation.

The best thing that came out of that summer, aside from that book, was a conversation I had with someone from Australia about his travels to Thailand, China, and three other countries! I yelled, "how could you afford that?!" He took his eyes off the road for a second, smiled and said "an around the world ticket." "What the hell is an around the world ticket?!" He explained that it was a multi-destination ticket you could buy and have up to a year to use. He told me that he would stay at each place for a few months at a time, get a job, and learn about the culture and the people. "How much is that?" When he said he paid $2,000 for that ticket I nearly jumped through the roof! I can pull that off!

I was hype!

I found a company and had Haiti, Peru, India and Tibet on my ticket but a price increase meant I had to kick Haiti and Peru. I pulled out a map to see what country I could go to that would be cheaper than Tibet but close enough for me to hop on a train. Hi, Nepal! This journey was about experiences, nothing about it was about work or money.

I reached out to a friend in India that I collaborated with a year prior about dance schools I could volunteer at. I found a school in India called The Shiamak Dance Academy that was amazing. They insisted on paying me but met me half way and allowed me to provide for less fortunate youth.

I also signed up for a WWOOFing network in Nepal (World Wide Opportunities on Organic Farms.) The money I paid would support the farm I was on, I'd learn a skill, about the people, and the culture. WIN! I would also volunteer at an orphanage (that was actually more like a foster home) while in Nepal as well.

I was abroad from that summer in 2013 up until mid-January of 2014. It changed my life forever. Being back in the U.S.A had me in a haze. We have so much and yet so little. I questioned everything but one the question I asked the most was, "why did I choose to come back here?" and by "here" I mean back on this earth! "Why did I choose to be born? It's so hard here!" Then to that you add: being a woman, being black, being a lesbian, a foster child, an artist, being tall, being an entrepreneur.... Why the hell did I come back into this game of life?!

Your spirit is your best navigation. Your true-self is the best driver.

Being in another country as an American or a tourist and being seen as a dollar sign was an awakening experience for me. I was stared at every single day I lived in Nepal. It was nuts. My blackness was unreal to them. Being there was also unreal to my friends, but the lesson was bigger than being stared at. I learned how much I was lied to about other countries "needs" from Americans, and reminded how the saying "treat someone like you would want to be treated" is another misconception.

While in India, I spent most of my time with affluent people who walked by beggars with less attention than you'd give a stranger, even when they followed us for blocks! They told me "they are beggars by choice, it's their profession." It's how they get by, just like a person working at Pizza Hut or a law firm. I learned so much about how hard EVERYONE in that country works and how they prioritize their spiritual well being. Observing that level of self-care was significant as an American.

<3 <3 <3

"ONE MAN'S TRASH IS ANOTHER MAN'S TREASURE" – SOMEONE IN THESE STREETS

Traveling always seems to remind me in the RAWEST way how much I actually have from physical things to the material things to opportunities. Visiting other countries has showed me how much I can do with even less. For everyone it will be different, but anyone will benefit from strategically expanding outside of his or her usual surroundings. I used all the money I made from camp and the bit I made while in NYC to take that trip. I had NOTHING when I got back to Miami, but I would have never known to what length my friends supported me had I not followed my intuition, made a choice, known what I wanted, and went for it. I learned that I had more support than I ever imagined.

> *"YOU MISS 100% OF THE SHOTS YOU DON'T TAKE."*
> *– ANOTHER SOMEBODY WE DON'T KNOW*

Most people talk themselves out of things way before considering ALL the options. You always have options and you always have a choice. If your intentions aren't set, if your belief isn't there, and your willingness to take actions or to take the initiative isn't there then NONE OF THE SUPPORT WOULD HAVE SHOWN UP. What would there be to support? Doubt? NOPE! If you start off small, you can build yourself up.

Travel wasn't something I was thought was a benefit, but it has a power to direct and redirect you on your path. It opens your mind and feeds your soul. Funny enough, passports are stamped, leaving you with a physical reminder of your travels and so it is with your soul. Every place you visit leaves an imprint and adds texture to your personality, makes you more interesting, and provides you with more to offer humanity and every person you meet. As a foster child, on a daily basis you are reminded that change is the only constant in life, so why not apply that to your movement in your own way and on your own terms?

When you look to your past, you realize you're always on the right path.

Truth Through the Pen

1.   List 12 places you want to go in this lifetime. (When you write it, know it's possible. If you don't have that feeling, come back to this when you do.)

El Salvador, Trinidad + Tobago, Italy, Dubai, India, China, Japan, Iceland, Mexico, Cuba, Himalayas, New York

2.   Pick 6 of those places and share why you want to go there.

- El Salvador to get in touch w/my roots
- T+T to see Dijah's roots + family
- Dubai party capitol, very rich
- India to see how people work/live
- Himalayas to live w the monks
- Japan to see how people work + live

Passport & Borderlines

3.   How do you feel about where you live now?

Uninspired, trapped, limited. I just
need to get out.

4.   Where has been the most interesting place you've been
so far? What was most interesting and why?

Long beach California. It felt like everyone
was living their life to enjoy it, not just
to pay bills etc.

5. What is the most amazing thing you have to offer to the world at this point in your life? (Remember, "the world" can simply be YOUR WORLD, either way greatness vibrates.)

I can commit to something I believe in
and I look outside the box for
opportunities

6. Life is a long message; if you don't listen, you will be lost. What was the last thing you heard?

"I know it will happen because I say so."

Passport & Borderlines

~~Picasso Phase~~

"WHEN YOU CREATE, YOU CAN MAKE ANYTHING."
– OWEN AZOULAY, 8 YRS-OLD

I felt like I wasn't heard, so I resorted to writing my thoughts in poetry. Five years later my poem "What Is Love" was published in a poem book. I will forever be proud. I can't find the copy of the book, nor have I been able to find it on Google since it happened way before that. But knowing something I created was seen, heard and appreciated enough to be recognized still gives me strength almost 20 years later.

When you realize you can make anything with your bare hands, the world is yours to mold. Like with all things, if you don't practice it, you WILL lose it. You will forget the creator in you.

cre • a • tor *(noun)*
   A person or thing that brings something to existence.

As humans, we're more attached to things we see than to things we don't. If you don't "see" someone for a long time, you FEEL like you miss him or her. If you don't "see" your things where you left them, you FEEL upset or worried. When you "see" your waiter coming with your food, you FEEL happy and excited. We are visually motivated, so physical things can often awaken feelings in us.

Picasso Phase

I found that when I created physical works, it helped me to unlock and open things within me. I've seen it work for many like this. Some of the most inspirational and powerful artists are those whose work to reflect who they truly are and what's happening in and around them.

Everything we do is some form of language, and like someone who is multilingual, the more languages you speak, the more people understand you. Art, in all mediums, has been a huge lifesaver for me. I don't know how I would have gotten by in foster care or during my childhood if I didn't find poetry and dance.

I found poetry at 11. When I was growing up, having a diary was the popular thing to do. After many attempts at jotting down my day to day, I got bored. I already had this dialogue in my head, why do I need to write it out too? Though I learned about the power of writing your wants, dreams, and thoughts down later in life, my diary quickly turned into a poetry book. I didn't read poetry, but it did appeal to me. It was an art and a challenge. How do you find words to rhyme in the perfect way that also express how you feel and think? Poetry was engaging and I needed that. It made me feel special because not everyone can write poetry. Right?

Growing up, there was always someone that was treated special. With my grandmother, my younger sister was favored and always seemed to get the "yes" responses. In my foster home, the foster mother favored her son and the father favored the daughter, or just both. So many people individually made them feel special.

I never shared my poetry. We were each other's favorite and that was cool for me, most the time. Dance was also another thing that made me feel special. But like with my poetry, I didn't share it. I eventually shared both though. I loved the challenge poetry brought, probably since I seem to love a challenge, but I was also born in it and of it. Creation and the arts showed me that you could be challenged, loved, appreciated and special all at the same time. The most magical part was that these were things that I felt about myself while expressing my talent. I didn't get it then how I get it now but it soothed me, made me smile, and it was my happy place. I would write a poem, breathe deep, exhale and keep it moving. Keeping it moving got easier.

My foster mother would say, "she'll get over it" in the most not caring voice ever. It stung every time and I always wondered why she didn't care enough to help. She was wrong though, I would never get over it. I'd go through it, by exercising my ability to tell her and whomever else how the hell I felt, then closing the book. Creating physical works also helped me keep a timeline of where I've been and where I've come from. I'm able to click rewind on my life, revisit shit, and remember why I'm doing what I'm doing. Bigger than that, the more I created, the more I got to know myself.

I learned how many different things I could do and how much it helped me express and heal myself. I needed healing, real healing. You are the only one who can really do that for yourself; everything and everyone else are tools to support you. I didn't invest in what people thought about my poetry or dance that much, but compliments and their shocked reactions that I could do what I did felt AMAZING and did a lot for my confidence. Feeling seen is POWERFUL and EMPOWERING.

My Life

I was in my mid 20's, being a choreographer and growing a name for myself in New York City. I was having all the fun! Dance parties, bars, beautiful people, and my forever growing confidence. I had never been in love and wasn't thinking about it honestly, but it creeps up when you least expect it and often seems to happen with someone that's going to take you on a ride! I was caught and I knew from the jump I should've got off the line and kept swimming. We never do. We hang, *Emoji Eye Roll*. She and I danced together and did a bunch of stuff that I never allowed myself to do with anyone else before her. I dug it. I liked the PDA, the lunch dates, the invites to trips with friends, and the laying in bed until we had to get going. This relationship was cool, and though it wasn't official, I wanted it to be.

She took a trip out of town for work and I felt a shift. We hung out again when she got back and when she was dropping me home I let her know I wanted to be an official thing, but she said she wanted remain the same. I said "well, I don't," got out the car and slammed the door behind me. I didn't want her to see anyone else at this point, and felt like she might have been still messing around with her ex, who was a well-known male DJ. The feeling I had while she was away was still in my bones and my intuition told me to go to the doctors and get checked out. My body felt a little different.

Two weeks later, I got a call from the doctor's office. I knew that they only call if something's wrong. The nurse said, "your test results came back and we need you to come in to get treated for chlamydia." "WHAT? You can get that from a girl?!" I yelled out. "Uh, yes ma'am, you can. You can get it from anyone you are having sex with." I WAS DEVASTATED!

how THE hell did YOU do THAT?!

How could this happen to me?! I have never in my life had a disease! I felt so gross! So hurt! And so UPSET WITH HER!

I went over to my friend NYCole's house and told her and licked my wounds, and then I called that girl and went off on her! I went on to tell everyone not to invite her anywhere we went because I would most definitely lay her out. No one did, but it didn't help.

Not seeing her didn't do anything for me. I still felt betrayed, hurt, nasty, heartbroken, and angry. I felt so much, but then I reflected on how things started off so great and yet ended so terribly! In the end, you always think about the beginning. I created a piece for a performance about it. "Goodbye Love" displayed a relationship in reverse, starting from the painful end to the blissful beginning.

I remember watching the piece and feeling an immediate release. The whole piece was healing. I used 3 girls in the piece, two of whom were also going through love woes. One was very nervous about performing in the style I created for the piece. We persevered. We all supported one another, moved on from those relationships, and grew our careers ten fold! Also, the woman I would be with for the next three years physically, six years spiritually and who changed my life forever was in the audience that night. I said goodbye to old love and hello to new love at the same time and didn't even know it.

<3 <3 <3

We are creators, the limits on this do not exist. An artist in the 1500's, Michelangelo, is a great example of someone who put no limits on his artistic expression. He painted, was an architect, a sculptor and so much more. One of his most popular works is the sculpture "David," a naked dude. While learning Kabbalah, I read a story about him where someone asked him how he created the sculpture. He said, "it was already there, I just kept chipping away." MIND BLOWN!!!

"GO INTO YOUR PAST TO BUILD YOUR FUTURE" – AFRICAN PROVERB, SANKOFA

Universal truth will always resonate with you; that statement made so much sense to me. Everyday we are chipping away at ourselves. Each day shows us a new version of ourselves and a hint at our true potential. A missed hit doesn't ruin the whole piece, it just creates a new path. We all have negative and positive traits, and each chip will make one shine more than the other. Michelangelo went on to be regarded as one of the greatest artists of all time. I don't know if that was his goal, but if he never allowed himself to explore his potential as a creator, he would have never become the creator he was... WORD!

Fun fact- Pablo Picasso used to burn his paintings to keep warm in his early years! The benefit of any struggle is your ability and motivation to be creative.

There is no greater example of this than Blacks in America. From the beginning of African history in America, oppression, bigotry, racial violence, murder, and more have been the order of the day. Despite or perhaps because of it all, Blacks have created as a form of healing and freedom. For centuries Blacks have been the architects in chains, physically and mentally, building what we know as America. Nothing has been handed to blacks, not even "reparations." Though this example is on a grander scale, talking about an entire people and their struggle, there are some aspects that parallel the abuse experienced by youth in the foster care system. Creativity is our freedom fighter! Creativity is how we defend our dreams. Your creativity is how you transcend oppression and utilize your struggle.

When I was in foster care they gave me a therapist, I couldn't stand what they stood for. "What!? Am I crazy!?" I knew I was more misunderstood than crazy. During each session I asked him about his day, what he had for dinner, and to play board games. In retrospect, I thought I was smarter than the therapist and that I was somehow beating the system. I now realize he was doing some creating of his own. The fact that I vividly remember those visits proves that the doc understood that I needed to feel some type of control and comfort in the space. He knew I wouldn't give him anything in a traditional therapy session or being approached in a traditional way. He gave me a space that provided what I needed.

What's good for the goose ain't always good for the gander!

It's hard to look around and see that the same things are seemingly working for everyone. Everyone seems to be going to college, everyone seems to be getting good grades, everyone seems to be in relationships, everyone seems to have a big happy family, everyone seems to learn the same. Getting caught up in comparison will always be a loss. Once you tap into and engage with the creator in you, you will begin healing, self-soothing, figuring out what works for you and how you shine. How can someone that's not you be able to tell you who you are? An even more important question is: when someone asks, "who are you?" will you be able to answer?

how THE hell did YOU do THAT?!

Truth Through the Pen

1.   List all the ways you express yourself. (Ex: words, art, etc.)

_____

_____

_____

_____

_____

2.   List all the ways you wish to express yourself

_____

_____

_____

_____

_____

Picasso Phase

3.   Think about the last time that you used your creativity to get past a challenge.

_____

_____

_____

_____

_____

4.   List 6 life experiences you want in the next year.

_____

_____

_____

_____

_____

5.   Like Picasso, you will have to make sacrifices to support your purpose and your dreams. What comforts have you sacrificed lately?

_____

_____

_____

_____

_____

6.   As a creator, every moment is an opportunity to create and transform an idea into a reality. Are you doing it often enough?

_____

_____

_____

_____

_____

Picasso Phase

~~The Alchemist~~

"WHETHER YOU'RE IN THE KNOW OR NOT, I'M GOING TO GET MINE."- ANITA DAVIDSON, 29 YRS-OLD

All these things are simply preparation. That trip on the sidewalk is preparing your eyes to see the next crack in the floor. That burned hand is preparing you to take better care next time, and that failed relationship is giving you awareness to give appreciation to the next. Whether you realize it or not, you'll get something from each experience. You'll get what you need and you'll bring that lesson to life.

I hid my ability to dance and sing for most of my life, until I didn't. Year after year, compliment after compliment, I began to open up and share my talents, mostly in dance. And even though I wanted to put myself out there, I was really shy. Once I joined the social justice organization named "Council for Unity," I found a way to share with a purpose. I was a high school junior at the time and we went on trips to work with special needs youth. It was awesome.

My teacher encouraged me to do the talent show for the kids. I performed a one-woman dance to a Janet Jackson song. I was exhausted after three minutes of hard dancing, and no air conditioning whatsoever! I completed the five-minute song though. I couldn't stop! After the show, several children asked for my autograph which was so dope!

A few years later, I became a dance teacher, which I initially hated. Janet Jackson was my biggest inspiration, my first and only idol. I wanted to dance for her! I started teaching as a way to make money while I auditioned. During that time, I was picked up by the KR3T's Dance Company in Spanish Harlem and got the job through the director, Violet. I learned so much about being a better dancer there and danced alongside some of the top dancers in NYC. I became a principal dancer soon after joining the company, which meant a part of my re-sponsibility was to teach choreography to newcomers. It was fun when they knew what they were doing!

One humbling teaching experience involved a new, discom-bobulated, slow-learning dancer named Carlos. Patience was never my claim to fame, but I helped Carlos grow to be pretty awesome. So much so that he became a principal dancer in the company after I left. Carlos and I remained friends, and he even came to a dance class I taught years later. Our commu-nication was off and on but always based on love. Thank God for Facebook!

One day Carlos messaged me to tell me that he just got booked to do a tour with the Broadway Musical "In The Heights," where he would be dancing and singing. I was so happy for him and congratulated him on such an awesome accomplishment. I won't lie, I definitely thought about how far he had come. He reminisced about how frustrated I used to get when teaching him and reminded me that I encouraged him to quit because he was a terrible dancer. He said, "I'm

how THE hell did YOU do THAT?!

"MY CEILING IS YOUR FLOOR"- HUMBERTO LEE,
43 YRS-OLD

After I said that to Carlos he began to surround himself with and befriended dancers that were better than him and who supported him. In 2011, I actually asked HIM to be a dancer in an NY Fashion Week Show that I was choreographing. He came to rehearsals but ended up taking another job. Good for him!

It still blows my mind that I, of all people, said something so ugly to him. He got what was meant for him from my discouraging words whether I knew it or not. Like an alchemist, he took those words, transformed them, and then manifested the people and experiences necessary to foster the type of growth he was seeking. Whether he knew it or not, he blessed me by reminding me of who I was. It was like eating a huge slice of humble pie.

to eat hum • ble pie *(idiom)*
  Is to apologize and face humiliation for a serious error.

al • che • mist *(noun)*
  Considered very early chemist whose work surrounded transforming base metals into gold.

man • i • fest • ing *(gerund)*
  The materialization of an indication or sign or thought.

Creating physical works helped to expand my mind and pushed me to consciously create the world around me. It works hand and hand with manifestation. As I write this, I'm thinking about the chalkboard wall I created on the walls of my apartment. I've always wanted to be recognized for the work I do with the youth. For the past year, however, that desire has been very strong. Now I know why. For many years, I moved halfway in my purpose because I didn't believe I was good enough. My actions were a reflection of my beliefs. You always know when you're not living up to your potential, by the way.

Being unwilling to be vulnerable was my biggest weakness. I was so caught up in my ego that I convinced myself I could do and be whoever I wanted to be - all by myself.

I could be so much further if I worked harder.

This is something I have said, and continue to say, to myself. But the truth is I needed to work smarter, learning to keep the best type of company and working with people who are more intelligent than me. It humbled me and made me better. It made me want more for myself but even more important, it made me realize that the people that "had more" weren't very different from me. They struggled, doubted themselves, experienced rejection, and endured pain too. And here I am, on their boat. Invited. Admired.

hum • bled *(verb)*
   Lower (someone) in dignity or importance.

(Moments where even with high confidence, self-worth, and knowing you're great— you realize you can STILL be better and NEED someone else to elevate.)

I decided I wanted more recognition because recognition means more opportunity to live in my purpose. I wanted that, but had no idea how that would happen outside of me doing the work and hoping that someone, somewhere would be impressed. My friend NYCole sent me a text months before her 30th birthday, "Girl, I'm about to be 30 and didn't make the Forbes 30 under 30 list!" It made me think, because my mentor and colleague, Tracey Robertson Carter, always said I could win any award and make any list, but it was never something I really believed.

NYCole has always been an inspiration to me because she's always been bold and always wanted to reach goals "normal" people never thought about. As she spoke, my mind faded and I started to think about this beautiful artist I met at Art Basel the year before. She was in her late 20's and a friend was curating her exhibition. I met her and we connected over the two days she was in Miami. I looked her up afterward and saw she had been making a real impact and that she also made a 30 under 30 list for ELLE Magazine.

NYCole sharing this mindset had lit so many bulbs in my head! I got some chalkboard paint, washed it across walls in my apartment and started writing my intentions down. Across one part of the board, I wrote in huge letters, "Award Winner, Octavia Yearwood." On another area of the wall I wrote, "30 under 30 list, 40 under 40 list, 30 under 30 list, 40 under 40 list" over and over again. Everything in the chemistry of my being began to conspire with all the other energies of the world. I didn't get attached to an outcome nor did I think about it everyday; but EVERYDAY I walked into my apartment I was reminded of what was already mine.

The act of believing is powered by knowing it's already yours.

It made me smile every time. Eventually, I won the American Express Award from Americans For The Arts, just months after putting my intentions on the wall. Three months after writing the "30 under 30 list, 40 under 40 list" I would be flying back to Miami from work travels because I had made my first 40 under 40 list– Miami's 40 under 40 Black leaders of today and tomorrow, Ayyyyyeeee!

How do you make a dollar out of 15 cents? Think about a dollar. Believe it will come, allow it to come freely, and only do things that will make that dollar come to you. Learning to tap into your spirit's power and utilizing the spiritual support you are surrounded by is your largest, most limitless resource. The spiritual support that surrounds you is a complete community that consists of God/The Creator/The Universe/Allah, whatever name you choose, your ancestors, angels, guides, and probably a host of others I'm unaware of.

I've earned that if what you want is what you need and if it's aligned with your purpose, then it's already yours. Also, are you ready for what you're asking for? Most of us don't consider that. That's completely "normal," it's human, you're human... Part human at least!

This conditioned human part of you clashes with the super you, the alchemist in you, the spirit self, the child self, your higher self! Your human self is continuously compromised by things and people around you like your parents, your friends, television, music, and your community. All these things effect what you think is real, fake, possible, or impossible. The human aspect of you is way more reactive than the alchemist in you. The human waits for things to happen. The alchemist creates and manifests their reality.

"PEOPLE CAN ONLY MEET YOU AS DEEPLY AS THEY'VE MET THEMSELVES." – SOME INSTAGRAM MEME

You mostly already know what you are seeking and have the power to change any situation into a beneficial experience. But, like an adult who scolds a child for something they too have done before, you forget. You forget power you have; the power you live in, operate from, and tap into continuously. The alchemist is YOU! Your spirit is the key and the best navigation you could ask for! Some call it "following your gut." They make it so mystical and maybe it is a bit magical, but it is very much YOU.

"ALL THINGS HIDE IN THE LIGHT, YOU FIND TRUTH IN THE DARKNESS." – SOME ALIEN ANIMATED YOUTUBE VIDEO

If you see yourself somewhere in your life and you believe you can be there for real, then you will. Slavery offers one of the best examples of seeing yourself somewhere, tapping into the source and working for it. Slaves sang, they visualized, knew what they wanted, endured suffering, and saw freedom. If there is any REAL doubt in your being about it, that doubt will manifest. You can be nervous, you can even question— Actually, question EVERYTHING! Questions always bring answers, but don't forget you have the answers already. Allow for things to reside within something outside of time: your magic. We created time after all!

Vision is a funny thing. Some have 20/20 vision, known as perfect vision, and others need glasses, LIKE ME! People look into the sky and see kittens in the clouds, and others look into the sky and see a gun. Regardless of what you see, being able to see is most important. If you walked through your day not even seeing the sky, how beautiful would your days be? How much would you appreciate the sky? The more I became in tuned with my spiritual support system and my super self, the more I saw that cloud forming into the kitty, and the more I got in touch with what I couldn't see, the more I saw.

how THE hell did YOU do THAT?!

Truth Through the Pen

1.   What was the last thing you manifested in your life? (Nothing is too small. Ex: you thought about wanting pizza and someone offered to buy you some, etc.)

_____

_____

_____

_____

_____

2.   What do you want out of this life? (List all things from love, to family, to a career, to friends, to whatever else matters to you. Think as HUGE AS YOU CAN.)

_____

_____

_____

_____

_____

3.   How often do your actions promote what you want out of this life? What are those actions?

_____

_____

_____

_____

_____

4.   Do you have a place (a wall, a book, etc.) where you write down things you want to manifest?

_____

_____

_____

_____

_____

5.   If not, what would it be? If so, what is it and why did you choose it?

_____

_____

_____

_____

_____

6.   There are only three reasons you don't have what you want: It's not for you. You're blocking yourself from it. It's not time for it. Acceptance is the key. How often do you use it?

_____

_____

_____

_____

_____

The Alchemist

~~Why Do We Fall in Love?~~

"LOVE IS IMPORTANT AND GOOD, BECAUSE IT HELPS PEOPLE." – KELVIN PULIDO, 9 YRS-OLD

And so I bare my soul freely because I understand it's not for me to hold.

What does love have to do with it? The one thing I avoided most through life is what life is actually all about. How though? Love seemed to be the root of all my woes. It brought me here. It's what I felt I lacked the most. NO ONE wanted to give it away and it seemed to cost the most. Love came with the most pain and was the reason for all my tears. Love was vacant like empty calories, making you feel full while doing nothing for you, yet adding pounds, making you look and feel heavier to everyone around you. Love was a one-size-fits-all blanket that was meant to cover friends, family, work, and romance. Basically everything that matters in this world, but at night never seemed to keep all parts warm. That blanket never completely fits, bringing these cold drafts that leave you rudely awakened. I NEED A BETTER BLANKET BRUH! I wanted nothing to do with something that left me so compromised and so vulnerable. Love hurts, I'm good!

LOVE IS AN EXPERIENCE

As a younger girl, this thing called "love" proved to be nothing more than a pain in my ass, and obviously something too hard to achieve. No one did it "right," so much that I didn't know how to do it myself! How the hell do you love? I didn't try to figure it out. After all, so many had hurt my feelings trying. I wanted to spare people, so I walked through life with love on my "do not call list." I wouldn't say it to people, but I automatically melted when it was said to me... Don't get crazy, that wasn't often but I am sure if more people knew its effect on me, it would have been used more. I didn't know why the word had so much power over me, but probably because of how much I wanted it and how little I heard it.

The wrong type of love for you has the uncanny ability to draw you away from your purpose. It's up to you to realign yourself.

I didn't know how to make sense of love. Everyone did it differently. Some showed it through gifts, some through sex, others through nice words, some through smacking one another around. Some showed it through verbal abuse, some through cheating, and some through providing a lifestyle of comfort. It was crazy! How could love hurt someone tremendously and yet bring him or her so much happiness and joy?! Noooo thank you!

The only safe space where love seemed to exist but never had to be spoken about was in friendships. Friendships had great

how THE hell did YOU do THAT?!

Perks. My favorite part was how powerful I felt in them. If it wasn't working out for me, I could always kick them to the curb. That was something I couldn't do with family, but what family could do to me. I exercised that power like a dictator, kicking out anyone from my life that hurt my feelings. Fortunately, true friends were my first introduction to what real love is and they taught me why love is so important. My grandmother loved me, yes. She is no longer here with us, yet I still feel her love daily. My friends version of love made me feel safe, considered, understood, cared for, appreciated, wanted, fun and FREE. Because of that, I dedicated all my love to my friends. Not romance, not family, just friends. What was that anyway? I began to build this great wall way before I realized it. Having friends taught me what love was, but the first time I allowed myself to be in love with someone was when my whole life changed.

I held onto my virginity until I was nearly 21. Aside from being raised mostly by my grandmother that shamed sex and growing up seeing how sex complicated so many relationships, I held on to my virginity. I didn't want to be a stereotype. I honestly never cared about any boy I had an experience with. Not sexually at least. I was always a sexual person but I never let it get as far as sex. I was proud to be a virgin, and I never felt like I was missing out on anything when my friends lost theirs. I loved hearing the stories, though. "Tell me what happened!"

Once I got to be 21 I just didn't see the point in having it anymore and chose to lose it. If it wasn't going to be like some romantic movie where I'd be swept off my feet, fuck it! I didn't get why I couldn't get emotionally attached or connected to any guy I dated and I didn't want to wait for that anymore. By the time I choose to lose my virginity, I knew a lot about sex.

Why Do We Fall in Love?

It was pretty disappointing. I would go nearly a year before I even tried it again.

My attraction to women would be explored throughout that time, mostly in thought. It took some time and acceptance before I realized that I was never attracted to men was because I was a lesbian. It would still be four years after losing my virginity before I would meet a woman that I allowed myself to fall in love with. I would learn a lot from that on-again-off-again relationship for many years. The love that grew in that relationship will never die and will always be appreciated. And I don't mean that in any cliché way.

"WHY DO WE FALL IN LOVE?!" Love is the realest, most impactful thing you will experience because it is YOU in the raw. True love is wellness. Love, in all forms, is a huge mirror! That's why people love so much! WHO DOESN'T LIKE LOOKING IN THE MIRROR!?

SIIIIIIKKKKKKKKEEEEEEEE!

This is why it can be such a messy experience. If you look in the mirror and don't like what you see, you will do one of two things. Maybe more but in my opinion: 1. You will avoid the mirror completely, losing all sense of yourself. How lost you'll be will depend on how long you choose not to look at yourself. 2. See your beauties and flaws and love them all. It takes a lot of work to look in the mirror and see new things to appreciate and to work on. The work will be never ending. It's literally like when you stand naked in the mirror, after months of working out and say, "ugh, I wanna get rid of that roll! Aw man, is this stomach ever gonna be flat?"

Just like a body transformation, you will barely see the day-to-day progress, but you will feel it. You'll notice you have more energy, you'll be happier, your clothes will fit a bit looser, then like out of nowhere - you will see that six pack peek out! It's the same type of thing with self-growth and improvement. There is no quick fix. Love is the key but like anything...

THERE ARE LEVELS TO THIS!

Falling in love with someone else taught me how to think about someone else before myself. The relationship's end taught me how much I didn't know myself. Love allows you to take responsibility for the part you played because the act of romantic love is a collaboration. I was so used to doing things alone, but love is inclusive. I was also responsible for it ending. The relationship's demise also made it very clear that I had a lot of work to do on myself. I am someone who does not like to make the same mistake twice, so the journey to learning myself is consistently a humbling one. The same lesson will come in different forms until you learn it.

MAKING THE SAME MISTAKE IN LIFE IS EASY!

The more I got to know myself, the more I surprised myself. WHO THE HELL AM I? Learning who I am never fails to take me on a ride that leaves me saying, "I never thought I'd be doing this." Being on this journey brings me back to being a child. Every turn is exciting, interesting, scary, and keeps me in the present. Being present is such a game changer! Being present allows you to realize your blessings and visualize all you

Why Do We Fall in Love?

want to manifest. "First times" are never ending! Through falling in love, the relationship ending, and having awesome friends, I was inspired and supported through a journey of self-discovery.

> *"BECAUSE THE ONE THING YOU WANT TO DO IS TO LOVE, AND THAT LOVE SHOULD BEGIN WITH YOU. ONCE YOU LOVE YOU, YOU LOVE THE WHOLE WORLD." – DR. SEBI*

As much as falling in love was the catalyst for a HUGE TRANS-FORMATION within me, I would not have been able to fully explore it if I was in a relationship the whole time. I had to do it alone. Love opened me up. Reading books about philosophy by spiritual leaders and watching different videos and documentaries helped me see from different perspectives. Mind blown again and again! When it resonated with me, I knew it was the truth. Anything resonating is a sign of remembering.

The fear of truth was a major hindering factor in my life. I feared lack of support, lack of love, and lack of ability so much that I rarely allowed myself to receive or even give these things. Learning to love myself quickly chipped away at fear. Self-love introduced me to the practice of *Self-Care* and *Self-Awareness*. Without either, self-love would have always been at risk.

hind • ering *(gerund)*
   Create difficulties for (someone or something), resulting in delay or obstruction.

Practicing self-care keeps you on top of your needs. I find that we live in a world where we constantly do for others. Service is important and at the forefront of the human experience on a daily, but there is not much you can do for others if you're not good to yourself. Being good and kind to yourself is number one, always! When thinking about anything lasting, you have to consider sustainability. How can you sustain living in your purpose if you don't feel good and think great things about yourself?

Practicing self care makes you consider yourself like you would consider others. If you're hungry you'd say, "I'm hungry. I'm going to stop this and go eat before I get hangry," or "I feel so drained, I'm going to take the day off." "I'm going to make sure I meditate daily to maintain spiritual balance and clarity." Whatever it might be, practicing self-care makes you do things that will make YOU happy which keeps you balanced.

Practicing self-awareness is like checking in on yourself. Self-awareness makes you ask yourself why you feel or act a certain way instead of blaming others. We love to blame others, don't we? This tool really gave me a lot of power. Read this carefully, because when you feel your parents have forsaken you. It's very easy to think everyone else will too! Self-awareness helps you discover what the problem is WITH YOU and what you may need to do to aid it. That check in or "Self Check" as I like to call it, is super important. "How am I feeling, for real?" Pay attention to how your body is reacting. Are you reacting or is this action a conscious choice? Is this choice beneficial to you, or is it from a fear-based place? Reacting is not conscious, which is why it often makes things worse. Without self-awareness, you're a walking reaction spilling onto everyone in every encounter.

We are misunderstood when we don't understand ourselves. Lacking understanding of why we feel what we feel or why we do what we do. Though there are some universal truths, there are a trillion other truths that apply to your specific situation, and it is up to you to figure them out. It will take time. It will take patience. It will take help. It will take love. It will take support. It will take openness. It will take courage. It will take willingness. You will go through it. You have to. And you will feel weak. You will feel powerful. You will feel exposed. You will feel vulnerable. You will feel like a loser at times, but you will also feel like a winner. Allow yourself to feel. Instead of swimming in it, observe the waves. Observe what is happening and watch it pass. All of it always passes.

Love introduced me to self-care and self-awareness, and for that I am forever thankful. The best part about practicing self-awareness and self-care is how it reminds you of where your power lives.

Right in YOU! It's change- TAKE IT TO THE BANK!

People who make the most change are those who know they are worthy of better.

Truth Through the Pen

1.   Have you ever been in love? Who was your first love?

_____

_____

_____

_____

_____

2.   What was your best love experience? What made it so great?

_____

_____

_____

_____

_____

Why Do We Fall in Love?

3.   What did you learn about yourself being in love and what have you done to make yourself better for all forms of love in the future? (THINK)

_____

_____

_____

_____

_____

4.   Do you practice self-care or self-awareness? If so, in what ways? (List ALL WAYS)

_____

_____

_____

_____

_____

5.   How do you show that you take responsibility for the situations happening in your life?

_____

_____

_____

_____

_____

6.   If it doesn't go your way, I'm sure it was meant to be that way, but what part did YOU play?

_____

_____

_____

_____

_____

Why Do We Fall in Love?

~~REBEL WITH A CAUSE~~

"THE SKY IS FALLING; THE WORLD IS CALLING. STAND FOR SOMETHING, OR DIE IN THE MORNING" – KENDRICK LAMAR

January 8th 2014, 4:36am Kathmandu, Nepal

Here's the truth... With 3 days left until I return to the states, my deepest desire is to have found a cause to be passionate about. I wish that a humanitarian spirit that never really ran deep in me before would awaken, and that I will return to the states with a portable tap to screw into every person I meet! Alas... I stand here, A Rebel without a cause, instead.

I've been sitting with my thoughts trying to let it ferment and soak from the barrel I'm in, as much as possible, like wine. Instead, impatient, like a human, I have to pour out a taste of what I'm feeling in this very moment.-OhhhTumblHer.tumblr.com

"The Quitter never wins and the winner never quits"

REBEL WITH A CAUSE

I came across this blog post in my phone as I searched for a quote for the book. These words brought visuals, sounds, and smells, turning me into an instant time traveler. Life, being its sensory self, I was transported. For eight and a half months after that, I was in a jaded funk EVERY DAMN DAY. Everyday I questioned why I chose to come back to earth, this dimension. I carried a huge load of disappointment for the people of the world. "IT SUCKS HERE!!!!" "IT'S SO HARD HERE!" People called these places third-world countries, but after being immersed in their country, so much of the strife seemed to come from lack of unity and laziness. They want you to drop the rice and go. They don't really want your help. AMERICA LIED TO ME! Their third-world works for them.

When I was in Nepal, I was stared at everyday. Every Single Day. Africans weren't even allowed into the country. A woman who was there representing an African filmmaker told me this. Nepali people would ask me if I was Indian! That's how far fetched my blackness was. That wasn't the problem for me though, I am BLACK FROM AMERICA. What annoyed me most was how they rejected my efforts to learn about their culture and language. Bigger than that, I realized that my country had programmed me with mental rose-covered vision that said whole world was ugly and rolled around like a pig in mud. I WAS DEVASTATED. I never cared enough, but being exposed left me exposed.

I was fresh off of from going to a Vipassana Meditation retreat, to India, to Nepal, and to NYC with. I had virtually no money and no home to come back to when I got back to Florida. I had a few belongings in a storage unit;, but that didn't matter. The only thing that plagued my mind was how people only cared only about themselves, and howl was asking myself how I was going to figure out what my purpose was here. I understood why people took their own lives. After all, anywhere but here seems easier. This world is so dense. So hard. "Wtf am I supposed to do?!" It was really hard for me to be happy. I would be turning 30 soon and there I was feeling like I'm starting all over again, like I'm starting from scratch.

I sat in the backyard of my friend Yasmin's house in a daze, thinking about all that just happened in my twenties. It was so much! I've lived in almost every borough in New York City, in two cities in New Jersey, and four states all together. I've been to five countries, worked at many restaurants, bars, public schools, and dance studios. I sold drugs, slept on six friend's couches, and even on trains. I fell in fake love three times, lost my virginity, fell in real love once, lost a million pounds and then gained the million back. I've been a meat eater, vegetarian, and a vegan!

Now I'm 30!? I had never been terrified of aging before, but out of nowhere came the heat of a fire burning under my ass. I had no idea which way to go. I just knew I did not want to start over again. I didn't want to end up on another friend's couch, even though it was frequently by choice so that I could work on being better and achieve some goals professionally and personally. It was harder to do this with all the other distractions in the world. It was a humbling position to depend on others when I also wanted to reach these goals and sustain my lifestyle and independence.

Though I am weary of the ways of the world, there is no growth in comfort.

REBEL WITH A CAUSE

I meditated a lot. I spent a lot of time alone too. Hours on the phone with friends really helped to keep me above water. I rode my bike and walked sometimes. I had real-life conversations with myself and my spiritual support system. I continuously asked why and complained about being alive.

Nine months later, my friend and co-founder of a nonprofit asked me to be a guest speaker at the foundation's third annual fundraiser. A few years prior, I wanted to speak, but I never had the courage to ask. When she asked me, which seemed to be out of the blue, I was more than excited to say YES! I had no idea it was going to be the catalyst for a radical shift that brought me to this very moment in time: sharing with you.

I had only shared "my story" with those who were closest to me. Letting people in was not something I did often. 'Who cares about who I was and where I came from? Does that even matter? People are always using and looking for excuses. I don't want to be an excuse. I don't want a pity party, just take me as I am."

Thinking like that was also a big excuse. I thought I was being strong but it was my fear taking over. Not sharing anything was all about me being ashamed of my past and not wanting to be rejected. But after I spoke at the fundraiser, my whole life changed.

After I spoke, so many folks from reality stars to business owners came up to me sharing how impacted they were. Tommy Davidson, whose films and characters I grew up with was also a speaker that night. I introduced him and sang an excerpt his character "Vernell Hill" sang on my favorite show "Martin." He laughed so hard! We all did! Then he shared his story about

how THE hell did YOU do THAT?!

being left in the garbage and being adopted by a white family, then all of a sudden we were the same. It clicked to me! You share because it creates that space for that one person who feels alone to know they are not!

I got back to Florida, and while buying dance business cards I got an offer to get 100 free cards for something else. I hate to miss a deal, I reflected and said, "I want to be a motivational speaker!"

All these years, I was being selfish in the worst way and it was so easy! I was watching out for my feelings and not considering all those I could be helping along the way. Trauma, experiences, and memories are lasting and are so painful. Choosing to succeed and leaving the past behind you is a double-edged sword. People may hear your story and be inspired, but how are you being consciously inspirational? The following year, my friend Melissa did a card reading for me one day and said to me "You have to be the hope. You've been trying to inspire it, but you have to be it." She was translating the cards and channeling the message, but like all truths, it resonated with my spirit.

Not having an active mother, not knowing my father, my mother not knowing my father, my mother abusing drugs and alcohol, being in foster care, traveling from home to home with a black plastic bag as luggage, childhood stories of being left in a crack house, and remembering when I hid in a closet because my drunk mother came to our apartment banging on the door over loud music while my grandmother shouted at her to go away, was all shameful to me. There was a lot I was ashamed of, like almost getting myself raped when I got in a car with a man that said he was going to take me shopping for clothes. I had a lot of shame, but damn, what a way to prepare for greatness! What could better qualify me to be a source of hope? My fear made me subconsciously rebel against myself, causing me to hold myself back constantly, and I didn't even realize it.

"YOU GOT TEARS SO THEREFORE TECHNICALLY YOU'RE NOT DEAD" – MUHAMMED ALI

Two months after the fundraiser in December, I was asked to be the lead facilitator of a mentoring organization. I never considered mentoring a day in my life before that. The term in itself was pretty foreign to me. My initial intentions were to integrate my dance program because I was concerned about losing my identity with something new. Tracey Robertson Carter, the executive director, was so positive and upbeat and always got things done. I enjoyed that about the new atmosphere. She also valued my opinion and asked me for input.

Meanwhile, I've said I wanted to be a motivational speaker, I now had to do it, but I felt so conflicted. Sharing my story felt redundant and also, I doubted if anyone even cared. It felt too self-involved and I cared too much about what people thought. Would they think I was vainly into myself? There are so many more tragic stories out there than my own. Am I even that interesting?! This new path had to be about more than just me, but it had to be creative and done in a way that was unique to me. So, I made no moves. I had no moves.

Group mentoring gave me a platform to speak but also to listen. Listening to these young people's stories was the best part. Identifying with each of them was a constant occurrence. BLACK YOUTH. For so many years, I forced myself to connect more with my Latin side. I experienced more unification with other Latin people and I loved that! As soon as I spoke Spanish I was accepted and greeted with open arms. I think I rejected being black because being black is hard, but when I mentored I couldn't help but see myself in their looks, in their clothes, in their hairstyles, and in their stories.

Again, I was rebelling against myself, rejecting myself, doing to myself what I feared others would do to me. There was no way that I could continue to reject being black and turn a blind eye to all the elements that factor into generational hardships. My mentees are living the life I lived with a lot less support, so how the hell are will they be able to thrive in this world?

Muted! As a young person I felt muted. Artists like Michael Jackson, Prince, Oprah, and Maya Angelou were muted in their youth too, but found their voice through art. Then you have Muhammad Ali who used his voice a lot on the platform he had in boxing. There aren't many people who don't know the famous phrase "float like a butterfly, sting like a bee!" But his last few years on earth he too was muted by a disease. He had no idea this would happen but he surely stayed true to his purpose and his message for as long as he could, vigorously and boldly!

A childhood filled with adversity, heartbreak, disappointment, pain, hopelessness, hurt, darkness, fear, abuse, carelessness, poverty, and violence can leave you in ruins. Your world feels and looks like a war zone. This will happen until you make a real choice to rehabilitate your mental space. You have the right to rebel and be a rebel. After all, life isn't easy! More times than not, it leaves you feeling like a warrior in battle. But you have to be self-aware enough to know if you are fighting yourself and that you are not armed with weapons that can only hurt YOU.

reb • el *(noun)*
A person who rises in opposition or armed resistance against an established government or ruler.

My Life

I am a huge biography buff; reading the stories of others really fuels my spirit. When I was 9 or 10 years old, I either got to school late and couldn't get in those strict Catholic school doors, or I experimented with sneaking out of the school without getting caught. Either way, this day it took me on an adventure through Rockaway Park.

My grandmother made it a point to teach us how to travel to school and back on public transportation on our own. I couldn't get back into school so I walked in the direction of home. I stopped at a corner store to buy candy. I had a dollar, and while scoping my options, I saw Big Bol Gum, a candy coated bubble gum, for 1 cent! A penny! I was amazed! I bought 100 of those things!

My sister was with me. We ended up at a library. We figured we'd be safe and unfound, so we decided to stay there until it was time to go home. We found ourselves surrounded by books, and nothing else to do but eat gum and read, and so we read. The first biography I ever read was one on Oprah Winfrey. Although she was popular then, she wasn't the "Oprah" she is now. I became amazed by her struggles. I was reading every chapter like a movie and seeing that little girl as me, whoa! I quickly began to dislike reading, but years later, the words of Dr. Maya Angelou would strike the same cords in me. I found so much inspiration in their stories and the stories of so many others. The common theme always seemed to be trauma, pain and sacrifices thereafter.

"AT THE END OF PAIN, THERE'S SUCCESS."

– ERIC THOMAS

<3 <3 <3

You would think that after all types of abuse, and a childhood that lacked love from family, that would be enough! But the road to serving and living in your purpose is riddled with sacrifices. For example, monks renounce all material things in order to reach, or get as close as they can, to spiritual enlightenment. There are lists of people who have died and been killed as a result of living in their purpose. Perhaps that's why they call it your "life's work." All the challenges you have experienced in your life are a testament to your greatness, no matter how big or small. Those are sacrifices for the greater good in you. Everything is preparation! Never forget that! And never forget the sacrifices of those before you, like that grandmother who invested in you instead of ANYTHING ELSE she could have been doing. That parent that didn't fold when they had to do it alone, and that teacher that fed you when you didn't know when you would get your next meal, or that one friend who always made themselves available to you. Instead of counting your losses, count your blessings. Tally those joints up, I am sure you will realize you have a lot to pay back!

Have a sense of obligation rather than a sense of self-pity and entitlement. No matter how many times they call you "under-privileged," know that you are not. That statement creates a sense of entitlement, and long as you think something is owed to you, you won't work for it. Know you deserve it because of the work you've put in to be better and to do better.

en • ti • tle • ment *(noun)*
  The belief that one is inherently deserving of privileges or special treatment.

Paying back those people who have invested in me has been and continues to be a driving force within me. If there was a Sallie Mae for blessings, my phone would be ringing off the hook! I have been given so much in this life and this is why I want to give so much to you all through words, frequencies and LOVE. There is a lot to do in this world and we all have so much to offer. You have to ask yourself, "how can I be the solution?" and sometimes ask yourself, "how am I being the problem?"

Find Your Purpose, Rebel

The never-ending question: "what is the key to success?" The fact is that there are multiple, and they're all dependent on you. So many are "impressed" by my personal success and way of being, mostly because adverse childhoods make it hard to succeed. Why? Because people with traumatic childhoods rarely find true joy and happiness. Joy and happiness helped me identify my purpose. Your purpose is the cause within you where your joy is stored. Joy is where you pull your happiness from. It's no surprise that what you've been looking for all this time has been within you and is YOU. The virus is often used in the cure. Everything you have experienced is what you needed in preparation to get free and be the better you that you were meant to be. If you never forget this, you will forever be grateful.

I found my purpose when I stopped being ashamed and running from my past. Running from every reminder of the past seemed like the right thing to do until I started to unpack my baggage. Sifting through all the garbage takes so much time! I read an article the other week whose title read, "If Black Millionaires Won't Lift Us Up Then We Will."

Even the compassionate are blind

I feel like a high percentage of black millionaires are from poverty stricken backgrounds and single parent homes. Their focus probably being to escape the shortcomings of their past. Seeing that title resonated with me because if my focus was more about money than self growth, then I would not have realized how important it is to be very hands-on and consistent with youth that had childhoods like mine and worse. It's difficult to consider others when you are thinking about yourself.

Though selfishness gets a bad wrap, the world is lacking empathy. Harriet Tubman WALKED herself to freedom, and WALKED BACK countless times to help free others. She never forgot what it was to be a slave. I never forget how I felt, what happened, what I wanted, or why I wanted it. There is NO thought or thing "NEW" under the sun we're living under. What you need, needed, want, wanted, is the same for millions of others too. How will you provide? You are meant to be a part of the positive progression of humanity, so it is your obligation to help those in it. I owe a great deal of those I am to the youth I've worked with. Through them, I was reintroduced to what it meant to be empathetic. Working with youth in India it was humbling to learn that, unless their parents can pay for it, they won't get an education.

Not everyone is meant to use the arts to service the youth and humanity as a whole, like me, but everyone is here to GIVE. It's an OBVIOUS TRUTH. We are all here to give, receive, and spread the love and light that lives in us.

com • pas • sion • ate *(adjective)*
   Feeling or showing sympathy and concern for others.

The Rebel With A Cause Is a Revolutionary, Revolutionize!

The revolutionary will forge a lasting shift in the consciousness of everyone they meet. The revolutionary never dies! Their spirit will vibrate through and transfer from everyone they've met and onto the next. The revolutionary feeds limitlessly. Planting seeds to be harvested and dropping crumbs that lead the way. Turning water into wine, or one loaf of bread that feeds millions, the revolutionary creates in the most magical way, making EVERYTHING out of nothing.

rev • o • lu • tion • ize *(verb)*
   Change (something) radically or fundamentally.

how THE hell did YOU do THAT?!

Truth Through the Pen

1.   What can you give to humanity?

_____

_____

_____

_____

_____

2.   What do you love and care about most? Outside of the usual, family, friends, etc.

_____

_____

_____

_____

_____

REBEL WITH A CAUSE

3.   Name three people that inspire you and describe all the reasons why.

_____

_____

_____

_____

_____

4.   What excites you most about yourself?

_____

_____

_____

_____

_____

5.   Name 1 person you don't know who inspires you the most.

_____

_____

_____

_____

_____

6.   When was the last time you gave back to your community? What did you do?

_____

_____

_____

_____

_____

REBEL WITH A CAUSE

~~Epilogue~~

I'm almost 100 percent sure you've made it through this book a lot quicker than it took for me to write it. That there, is LIFE. Trillions of moments condensed into seemingly ONE thing— YOU. This book was written with you in mind, guided by and made possible by so many others, others that still occupy this earth and others that don't.

I recently watched a bit of the video where a few youth tied up and abused another, yelling "FUCK TRUMP!" in the background. The whole time I was watching, I was noticing how important it is to be better and give what you can to humanity. I stopped watching and said, "I need to finish this book, they need me." I saw hurt, pain, fear, exercising "power," confusion, lack of direction, lack of knowledge of their options, but doing what they felt they could. These moments change the course of life for so many, and so instantly. NOW IS THE TIME TO TIGHTEN UP! Save yourself with the WHOLE WORLD IN MIND! Sound daunting? Like too difficult a task? Please. Get through this, and let's make some shit happen.

I talk like this to myself and never doubt that I can I save the world. I really think I can. I suppose we'll see. The most amazing part about it is that there was a point in my life where I never even considered it.

USE THIS BOOK!

Epilogue

This book is meant to be a tool to get you to a destination. Log this into your spirit's GPS and take a ride. I made it short and hopefully you found whatever you needed in it. I used these tools, I adopted many philosophies, and slowly elevated my mindsets to a space that has helped me move forward with a huge-ass smile on my face. I've cried more tears than I can count, and my chemistry has shifted more than I knew possible. This is what it's all about. You can do it, just take it day by day.

THE HUMAN EXPERIENCE.

If you are unhappy, lost, or any of the intense feelings attached to your lower self, then please understand that these experiences are meant to be yours. If you are reading this book, now is the time for change. This book in your hand is not a mistake or a coincidence. You just took a ride with me. I named real people who really exist and are available for your well-being and my own. I shared with you some things you may not have known, and some that you might already have. I know for sure I made you laugh and I know it's possible that moments of reflecting on your own life may have made you cry. I asked you questions that you maybe never really asked yourself before and I expected you to answer them. I gave you this book and you gave me your time. All of these things exemplify what is required in this game of life. These never-ending dualities serve as a reminder that everything is temporary and that you will always need both the ying and the yang, both the good with the bad, and the pretty with the ugly. The best thing to do is to avoid identifying with only one by knowing that you're both.

WHICH EXPRESSION WILL YOU LIVE IN THE MOST?

I was a foster child and I am queen, I was poor and I am wealthy, I was ugly and I am beautiful, I am everything. My mother left me in a crack house and my friends had me in penthouses. In kindergarten, I had a crush on a redheaded boy and also a girl. I have choreographed many dance performances, and now I'm writing a book for you. The best thing I did was live in my full expression, allowing me to be all that I am. You are not a singular being; you are multi-faceted. Every time you allow yourself to express all that you are, your positive vibrations are echoing through the world!

WHATCHUUUU DOING HERE!?

Let's tap in, let's tune in, and let's tune out all the things that don't benefit you or help humanity in any way! If there's one thing this book proves, it's that you can't do any of this alone. There is no real growth or progression that can be done alone. You have to keep humanity in the forefront or we are doomed. Start a circle of folks that are likeminded and have open discussions, real discussions about what you all want to do and how you can assist and collaborate to do it. Stop lying to yourself: you weren't born alone and you won't die forgotten.

BE BOLD! If you are moving with good intentions and for the betterment of more than just yourself, don't take on the negative perception and opinions of others. Throw all that in the tank, your spirit's gas tank, and drive yourself forward. Never forget that forward is forward and you will always make it to your destination. Never forget that the reason you look back on things is as a precaution for the future and also to know where you've already been. What you see when you look back will continuously be different from what you see when you look forward. Also accept that sometimes when looking forward you can't see shit! Granted that's scary, but on the road, there's always more road.

Being afraid of life is being afraid of yourself. You are creating it after all. Learn to trust yourself and learn to love yourself. Know the difference in the way you express yourself when you love yourself. Like yourself, dislike yourself, and hate yourself. Do self check-ins at every bend, and at every bend know that it all points back to you. Ask yourself why you are feeling something, stay away from blame even when being provoked. Remember, you have the power. Your heart and mind are tools- exercise them with meditation. When trials and tribulations arise, first find silence and be still, then make waves.

> *"YOU CAN THROW A BED IN ROARING WATER AND NOT SEE A DIFFERENCE, BUT WHEN YOU THROW A PEBBLE IN STILL WATERS, YOU WILL SEE WAVES RIPPLE INTO THE HORIZON." – SOMEONE IN A FILM I WATCHED*

Silence in a room full of noise is the loudest. The more you quiet your mind, the more you can hear messages for the creator and your spiritual supports. The more you quiet your mind, the more you hear YOURSELF and begin to build that trust within yourself to make AMAZING discussions.

You have the answers. You are the cure.

how THE hell did YOU do THAT?!

The best thing that happened in my transformation was the realization that "Child Octavia" is forever and "Adult Octavia" was her reaction to the experiences in her life. I couldn't be more thankful for all those experiences, friends and art for helping me free "child Octavia" from the cage. I want to ask that if you are reading these words right now, that you go and rescue the True You from bondage. She or he is a treasure being hidden, keeping you away from your greatness. The alter will never know you like the child will. The alter only knows how be what it is, a reaction, and its super power is self-sabotage. It's unconscious but it's up to you to be aware. No excuses from now on.

How do I get aware and stay aware?

ANSWER THOSE QUESTIONS at the end of each chapter, every single one, and then ask yourself some more. "Question everything" was some of the best advice a stranger told me. In the end, answers only exist because the question was asked! Everything is for a purpose, and life is a game so you have to play to win in order to receive the support you need and deeply desire. This book is meant to show and prove that everything that has happened before is in service to the NOW. There is no big mystery. The mystery only exists if you're not paying attention. For instance, these chapters, not the words in the chapters, but the color the chapter's titles are in. It is not like that because I'm gay! It's because each chapter I created symbolizes a part of your spiritual balance connected to your chakras. Each chapter's color is connected to that chakra, and like chakras, you can be closed if you put a lot of work into it. You can also be open by practicing or working on it. You can even be overactive by going from one extreme to

Epilogue

the next. EVERYTHING MATTERS! Below, you will find the chakras colors, titles, and meanings. Go back and review and do a self-check to see how your spirit reacted to each chapter and dig a little bit more as to why. Did that chapter excite you? Did that chapter overwhelm you? Was that chapter underwhelming? Did you just not get or understand that chapter at all?

Explore yourself, ask yourself the questions and watch yourself answer it. Attract it from others or bring experiences that answer it.

how THE hell did YOU do THAT?!

1.   The Root Chakra – The Sanskrit word for this Chakra is Mooladhara Chakra (mool means root). The chakra color associated with the root chakra is Red. The root chakra defines our relation to Earth. It impacts our vitality, passion and survival instincts. The red chakra colors are also indicative of our need for logic and order, physical strength and sexuality as well as the fight or flight response when faced with danger. The sense of smell in the human body is connected to the Root Chakra. The gland to which the root chakra is attached is the Gonads.

2.   The Sacral Chakra – The Sanskrit word for the sacral chakra is the Swadhisthana chakra. The chakra color associated with sacral chakra is Orange. Swadhisthana chakra relates to the water element in the human body. The chakra color orange impacts sexuality, reproductive functions, joy, desire and even creativity, compassion for others etc. The sense of taste is associated with the Sacral Chakra. Glands and organs impacted by this chakra include the lymphatic system, female reproductive organs, large intestine, pelvis, bladder etc.

3.   The Heart Chakra – Anahata Chakra, or the heart chakra, is associated with the chakra color Green. This chakra influences our relationships and has the Air element. A weak heart chakra is responsible for sabotaging the relationships through distrust, anger and envy etc. Sense of touch is impacted by the heart chakra and the glands connected to it are thymus and lymph.

4.   The Throat Chakra – The Vishuddhi chakra refers to our true voice. As the name suggests, the Throat chakra with its chakra color Blue is associated with the ability to communi-

Epilogue

cate, listen etc. The glands to which the Throat chakra is attached to are the esophagus, ears, throat, thyroid, jaws, teeth and neck vertebrae. The ethereal element of the Throat Chakra, when balanced, allows an individual to have a pleasant voice, artistic abilities, expressive ways, and also the ability to be in a higher place spiritually. The individuals with a balanced throat chakra are able to meditate well and use their energy efficiently and artistically.

5.   The Brow/Third Eye Chakra – The Ajna Chakra literally translates to "center of knowing or monitoring". This chakra is associated with the chakra colors Indigo and is connected to the Pineal or pituitary gland. Those with a well-balanced brow chakra can have telepathic abilities, charismatic personality, and they often do not have any fear of death. The element of electricity or telepathy along with the chakra color of Indigo are associated with our sense of Thought.

6.   The Crown Chakra – This chakra is known as Sahasrara chakra in Sanskrit and is associated with the chakra colors of violet or purple. The crown chakra is associated with the pituitary gland, nervous system, and the brain and head region with its element of light. In its balanced state, this chakra can render individuals the ability to perform miracles, transcend the laws of nature, and have a heightened awareness of death and immortality.

<3 <3 <3

The title of this book, "How The Hell Did You DO That?" is a question that I want you to be asked from this moment on. Be so great that you strike the curiosity of others and inspire their greatness. If you read this book and go off and emerge your-self in doing the work and transform your life, understand it is ALWAYS the beginning.

You are always learning and it is your responsibility' to attract the people and experiences that will prepare you for the next step in the greatness you outpour. The moment you lie to yourself and convince yourself that you don't need anyone and don't have more to learn; or that you are above anyone else, you will lose.

Epilogue

"YOU BETTER CHECK YO'SELF BEFORE YOU WRECK YO'SELF." – ICE CUBE

I just had the biggest intake and release that I've ever known...

Do not ever downplay your existence on this earth.... You are way more than you believe.

Hundreds don't know me, thousands by far, maybe millions unconsciously and yet I have... Without a DOUBT, changed the pace of their heartbeat.

I know it.

~~About the Author~~

O ctavia Yearwood is a former foster child. That's what stuck out about her the most while growing up. The growing pains attached to that is what has made her become all that she is now. Octavia Yearwood is you, on a different path.

Yearwood grew up in Queens, New York; where she was raised by her grandmother, Amy Yearwood, until she was 11 and went into the foster care system. She has since become an educator of various art mediums, a motivational speaker, a dancer, a radio personality, a recipient of several awards, an aunt, a great friend, an author, and whatever else she has set her mind to.

Epilogue

Yearwood's focus on foster youth and youth who have endured challenging childhoods comes from her recognition of how much her childhood affected who she is now. She fuels her support to youth to empower themselves and move past those blocks.

"I have more access than and the same ability as every leader that has come before me. I have a tremendous amount of work to do." – Octavia Yearwood